FREE Companion Resources and Videos Available

These **FREE** resources are perfect for individual use, parishes, small groups, and classroom settings.

- Weekly companion videos with Fr. Patrick Mary Briscoe
- *Witness Leader's Guide*
- Pulpit and bulletin announcements
- Downloadable flyers, posters, and digital graphics
- And more!

Scan here to access the free resources and videos or visit **avemariapress.com/pages/witness-resources**.

WITNESS

A GUIDED LENT JOURNAL FOR PRAYER AND MEDITATION

FR. PATRICK MARY BRISCOE, OP

Imprimi Potest: Very Reverend Allen B. Moran, OP, PhD
Prior Provincial of the Dominican Province of St. Joseph

Nihil Obstat: Monsignor Michael Heintz, PhD
Censor Librorum
Imprimatur: Most Reverend Kevin C. Rhoades
Bishop of Fort Wayne–South Bend
Given at Fort Wayne, Indiana, on October 20, 2025

Founded in 1865, Ave Maria Press is a ministry of the United States Province of Holy Cross.

www.avemariapress.com

Paperback: ISBN-13 978-1-64680-456-6

E-book: ISBN-13 978-1-64680-457-3

Cover and text design by Brianna Dombo Nicholson.

Printed and bound in the United States of America.

TO MY FATHER, A TRUE WITNESS.

CONTENTS

FOURTH WEEK OF LENT

FIFTH WEEK OF LENT

HOLY WEEK

FOREWORD

BY JONATHAN ROUMIE

Lent. Here we are once more—one of my favorite seasons of the year as a Christian. It is a time for meditative introspection, prayer, fasting, works of mercy, and sacrifice—all meant to draw us deeper into the mystery of the Lord's Passion, Crucifixion, Death, and, most eagerly, his Resurrection.

It is a story we know so well, filled with characters who humbly reflect every facet of our humanity—our flaws and our strengths alike. Lent invites us to take up the cross in communion with Christ so that grace may be found in the most unlikely of places. I cannot recommend its prayerful observance enough. Whether you are Catholic, Protestant, a follower of Christ's teachings, or simply a seeker of Truth with a capital *T*, Lent is a time for awakening, decisive action, boldness, and witness through charity and service.

Fr. Patrick Briscoe is a shining pastoral example of those very qualities.

In the summer of 2025, I had the honor, joy, and responsibility of bringing to the screen the reenactment of Christ's Passion, Crucifixion, and Death on the Cross in the sixth and penultimate season of *The Chosen*. I have portrayed Jesus in this series for eight years as of this publication—and without question, it has been the most important mission of my life. Fr. Patrick had a front-row seat to this particular season like few others. Yet he was not merely an observer—he was a committed prayer warrior.

Alongside my spiritual director, Fr. Patrick entered the trenches with me, helping to build the faith-centered foundation essential to my spiritual and mental well-being. In particular, he spent multiple days offering Mass at lunchtime for me and several cast and crew members during the filming of the scourging scenes—which, unbeknownst to many, were just as grueling on every conceivable level as the Crucifixion itself, though in different ways. His support helped me endure the physical and emotional toll of portraying those scenes and remain focused on what lay ahead.

Looking a little farther back—throughout the year and across several international trips, Fr. Patrick coordinated with my team so that Mass could be offered almost anywhere, at any time. Whether I was traveling for publicity tours or in the most grueling moments of my career portraying Christ, Fr. Patrick made every effort to ensure that Jesus was truly present and available to me, allowing me to draw strength from his Real Presence in the Eucharist. It was by that grace alone that I found the fortitude to carry everything God was asking of me.

The same dedication and tenderness Fr. Patrick has shown me throughout my journey reveals the kind of shepherd he will be on yours this Lent. He pours out his gifts in this Lenten devotional, *Witness*, through each day's meditations, reflections, and prayers. With his characteristic spiritual wisdom and grace, he turns our attention to the individuals—and, at times, the groups—who each played a part in the divine drama of Christ's eternal offering. In these pages, Fr. Patrick's devotion and insight invite you to step into that sacred story—to walk alongside those who were there, and to feel as though you could reach out and touch their cloaks.

It is truly my honor to offer these words of profound appreciation for what Fr. Patrick has done for me personally, and now, through this devotional, for all of you who are about to pray with it. I eagerly anticipate what our Lord and his Holy Spirit will do in your life as you journey through this beautiful and reflective season.

May you fully surrender to all that the Lord is asking of you this Lent. May these next forty days be a period of transformation, healing, and growing desire to conform your heart to his Sacred Heart. And may you seek what he wants for your life, not what you want him to do for you, so that your prayer may be "Less of me, Lord—more of thee."

In Jesus's name, may it be so. Amen.

INTRODUCTION

In recent years, *The Chosen* has done something remarkable—it has awakened a fresh curiosity about the life of Jesus. This crowd-funded series, with its cinematic storytelling and down-to-earth dialogue, has drawn millions into the world of the gospels in a way that feels real and immediate. People are asking new questions: What was Matthew really like? How did Simon Peter wrestle with his own weaknesses? What did it feel like for Mary Magdalene to be freed from darkness?

For many viewers, it's been a kind of rediscovery. These aren't just holy cards or vague memories from Sunday school—they're flesh-and-blood people with personalities, struggles, hopes, and flaws. Watching them wrestle with faith, friendship, and fear makes it easier to imagine our own place in the Gospel story.

The words of Ven. Fulton Sheen ring true: "The most interesting drama in all the world is the drama of the human soul." Unlike the stars in their courses or the stones along the road, human beings have freedom. We can choose—to love or to refuse love, to follow Christ or to turn away. This is what makes the drama of the Passion so gripping. It is, at its heart, the psychology of a fall and a resurrection—not just for Jesus or his disciples two thousand years ago, but in each of us today.

And this is exactly the invitation of Lent. The season slows us down so we can walk more deliberately with Jesus toward the Cross. It invites us to enter the Passion not as distant observers but as participants. When we do, we discover something surprising: Every one of the characters in the Passion has something to teach us.

In the cast of Holy Week, there is a mix of saints and sinners, heroes and villains. Some follow Jesus all the way to Calvary; others turn away in fear or betrayal. Some recognize him instantly;

others cannot see him at all. Some act with love and courage; others lash out with cruelty or indifference. And if we are honest, we can find pieces of ourselves in all of them.

We are Peter, bold in our declarations of loyalty but quick to deny when the pressure mounts.

We are Pilate, torn between what we know is right and the fear of losing human approval.

We are the weeping women of Jerusalem, moved with compassion yet unsure how to help.

We are the Roman centurion, surprised into belief by the sheer force of what we witness.

We are Simon of Cyrene, drawn into the suffering of Christ when we least expect it.

The Passion is more than a historical account—it's a mirror. In its scenes, we see our own faith tested, our own love revealed, our own hearts laid bare before God. Drawing from the Church's rich tradition, we can imagine what may or might have been and freely examine our own hearts. And in every encounter, we find the same Lord who turned doubters into disciples and sinners into saints still at work in the human soul.

This devotional will take you through the characters of the Passion one by one, looking at their choices, their failures, their moments of grace. Some will inspire you; others will unsettle you. But all will draw you closer to Jesus, the central figure who transforms the entire drama.

Because in the end, the story of the Passion is not only about what happened to him—it's about what is happening to us. Lent invites us to step onto the dusty roads of Jerusalem, to stand in the courtyard, to kneel at the foot of the Cross, and to watch the stone roll away. And in doing so, it invites us to let the miracle of redemption unfold again in our own lives.

HOW TO USE THIS JOURNAL

The *Witness* Lent journal's combination of daily meditations, questions for reflection, journaling space, prayers, and beautiful art is specially designed to draw you into a deeper, richer experience of Lent, preparing you not only to walk with Jesus to Calvary but also to go with him into the desert, to receive his healing mercy, to practice forgiveness, and to meet Jesus in the sacraments of Reconciliation and Holy Communion.

WHO IS *WITNESS* FOR?

This journal is for anyone who desires to enter more fully into the mystery of Christ's Passion and Resurrection. Whether you are a longtime Catholic seeking renewed fervor, someone returning to the Church after time away, or a new believer longing to know Jesus more intimately, *Witness* will guide you in daily prayer and reflection.

Witness is perfect for use in a group setting and was designed with that in mind. There's something special about taking this Lent journey with a community—whether that community is your entire parish, a small group, or your family. Visit www.avemariapress.com/pages/witness-resources for a leader's guide, help with organizing a small group, videos from Fr. Patrick Mary Briscoe discussing the theme for each week of Lent, and other resources to help you make the most of your time together with *Witness*.

You can also use this journal as an individual, with the meditations and journaling prompts helping you draw near to God, hear his voice in new ways, and pour out your heart to him as you turn your attention daily to Jesus's journey to the Cross. You may find that this Lent, you're in special need of regular, quiet times of connection with God; *Witness* is an excellent way to help you find that space each day.

HOW IS *WITNESS* ORGANIZED?

Witness is organized around six key virtues that emerge from the Passion narratives—virtues that Christ himself displayed and that he calls his disciples to embrace. Each week focuses on a different virtue, with daily meditations on figures from the Passion who embody (or challenge us to live) that virtue.

In Weeks 1 and 2, you'll focus on **Repentance** and **Trust**. We begin with the call to turn our hearts back to God and to place our lives in his hands, meeting those in the Passion narratives whose encounters with Christ brought radical change and renewed faith.

Weeks 3 and 4 dive into **Compassion** and **Humility**. We reflect on the self-emptying love of Jesus and those who stood by him in his suffering, learning to serve with gentleness, mercy, and unselfish care for others.

In Week 5, we examine the centrality of **Courage** in Christian life. As the Cross draws near, we look to those who followed Jesus even at great personal risk, asking for the grace to persevere when discipleship is costly.

The final week—Holy Week—calls you to contemplate the meaning of **Sacrifice**. We walk day by day with the central figures of the Passion, contemplating Christ's ultimate act of love and those who witnessed it, so that we may give our lives more fully in return.

Within each week, you'll encounter a simple daily pattern made up of the following parts:

Each day opens with a relevant passage from the Church Fathers, tying our present experience in the Church to our ancient past.

The meditation draws insight from a person or group in the Passion narrative, highlighting how their choices reveal the week's virtue.

The reflection challenges you to ponder and journal in response to the meditation, helping you identify practical ways to live out the Lenten season more fully. The benefits of journaling in this way are enormous—by putting your thoughts, prayers, and resolutions on paper, you take ownership of them in a fuller way, and they, in turn, have greater influence on you.

Finally, after you've read and journaled, the closing prayer provides a starting point for your own requests and prayers of thanksgiving and praise to God.

HOW SHOULD I READ *WITNESS?*

This Lent journal's daily format is flexible enough to accommodate any reader's preferences: If you're a morning person, you may want to start your day with *Witness*, completing the entire day's reading, reflection, journaling, and prayer first thing in the morning. Or, you may find that you prefer to end your day by using *Witness* to focus your attention on Christ as you begin to rest from the day's activities. You may even decide to read and pray as a family in the morning and journal individually in the evening. The key is finding what works for you, ensuring that you have time to read carefully, ponder deeply, write honestly, and connect intimately with the Lord in prayer.

Whatever approach you choose (and whether you decide to experience *Witness* with a group or on your own), be sure to visit www.avemariapress.com/pages/witness-resources for extra resources to help you get the most out of this special Lent journey.

WEEK OF ASH WEDNESDAY

Mary Magdalene

WEEK OF ASH WEDNESDAY

ASH WEDNESDAY

MAGDALENE MEANS "A TOWER" OR RATHER "BELONGING TO A TOWER," FROM THE TOWER OF WHICH IT IS SAID, YOU HAVE BECOME MY HOPE, A TOWER OF STRENGTH AGAINST THE ENEMY.

ST. BEDE

MARY MAGDALENE

Mary Magdalene's story begins in deliverance. Luke lists her among the Lord's closest friends, telling us a bit about the suffering she had known: "Mary, called Magdalene, from whom seven demons had gone out" (Lk 8:2).

We don't know what those "seven demons" were. Scripture leaves them unnamed. We might interpret them as fear, bitterness, pride, self-loathing, or even the pain of old wounds. Whatever had bound her, Jesus broke its power. His gaze reached her heart, and what once possessed her gave way to peace.

When evil is expelled, it seeks to return, often more subtle and determined than before. But it dared not come back to her. Her heart, now filled with his love, had become a dwelling place for Christ alone. There was no room left for the darkness.

And that's the extraordinary thing. The Gospel remembers Mary Magdalene by what Christ did for her—not for the demons that once ruled her life.

Lent invites us into that same encounter: to let Christ love us into freedom, to allow him to drive out what binds us and fill the empty places within us with his own presence. The grace that heals also guards. Love itself becomes the fortress of the redeemed soul.

We are entering a season not of self-punishment but of surrender. This is the time to bring our hidden burdens into the light of his mercy. Christ alone has the grace to drive out what we cannot master on our own.

In Mary Magdalene, we see what it means to face Christ and remain before him. To love him so deeply that sin loses its hold. To live so fully in his light that no demon dares to return.

REFLECT

1. What "demons"—fears, wounds, or habits—most often hold me captive, and how might Christ's gaze free me from them this Lent?
2. Mary Magdalene's deliverance was lasting because her heart became filled with love. What would it look like for my own heart to become so full of Christ that there is no room left for darkness?

PRAY

LORD JESUS, YOU LOOKED UPON MARY MAGDALENE WITH MERCY. LOOK UPON ME NOW WITH THAT SAME GAZE OF LOVE. SHATTER MY PRIDE, WASH AWAY MY SHAME, AND MAKE ME UNAFRAID TO STEP TOWARD YOU. DRIVE OUT FROM MY HEART EVERY EVIL THAT WOULD KEEP ME FROM YOUR LOVE. AMEN.

WEEK OF ASH WEDNESDAY

THURSDAY

WHEN OUR LORD SAW NATHANAEL, HE GAVE EXCELLENT TESTIMONY ABOUT HIM, THAT HE WAS NOT LIKE THE SCRIBES WHO WERE BEING DECEITFUL ABOUT THE SCRIPTURES, STRIVING TO ESTABLISH THEIR INTERPRETATIONS ACCORDING TO THEIR OWN WILL. HE SAID, "THIS IS A SCRIBE OF ISRAEL IN WHOM NO DECEIT IS SEEN."

ST. EPHREM THE SYRIAN

BARTHOLOMEW (NATHANAEL)

When we think of conversion, we often imagine a dramatic, sudden change, like Mary Magdalene. But the apostle Bartholomew (also known as Nathanael) reminds us that conversion sometimes begins quietly, with a single, honest question.

When Philip first told Nathanael about Jesus of Nazareth, Nathanael didn't pretend enthusiasm. He asked bluntly, "Can anything good come out of Nazareth?" (Jn 1:46). It's such a human response. Skeptical. Cautious. Honest. Nathanael's heart was sincere enough to admit doubt out loud.

But he didn't stop there. He accepted Philip's invitation: "Come and see."

That was Nathanael's first conversion. Not a change of belief just yet—instead a willingness to approach, to step closer, to see for himself.

When Jesus met Nathanael, he didn't shame him for his question. Instead, he honored it. "Here is truly an Israelite," Jesus said, "in whom there is no deceit" (Jn 1:47). Jesus saw in Nathanael what really matters: not a perfect person but a true heart. The Lord knew Nathanael wasn't hiding behind empty words or a public show.

And then Jesus revealed more: "I saw you under the fig tree" (Jn 1:48). We don't know what Nathanael was doing or praying under that fig tree, but Jesus's words touched something deeply personal. Nathanael responded at once: "Rabbi, you are the Son of God! You are the King of Israel!" (Jn 1:49).

From skepticism to proclamation—that's conversion.

For us, conversion often begins the same way.

Like Nathanael, we bring our true selves to Christ—doubts, questions, fears—and we let him meet us there. We say yes to the invitation: Come and see. And as we do, step by step, we become like Bartholomew: steady, faithful, and true to the very end.

REFLECT

1. How does Nathanael's blunt honesty in questioning Jesus challenge your own approach to faith?
2. Have you ever taken a step toward Christ before fully believing? What happened?
3. How can you grow in sincerity while still bringing your doubts to Jesus? What does "Come and see" look like for you in this season of Lent?

PRAY

LORD JESUS, YOU SAW NATHANAEL UNDER THE FIG TREE AND KNEW HIS HEART. SEE ME NOW AND MEET ME IN MY QUESTIONS, MY HESITATIONS, MY HOPES. GIVE ME THE COURAGE TO "COME AND SEE," TO WALK WITH YOU, EVEN WHEN I DO NOT HAVE ALL THE ANSWERS. MAKE ME A DISCIPLE WITH SINCERE AND STEADY FAITH. AMEN.

WEEK OF ASH WEDNESDAY

FRIDAY

THOSE WHO SAW HIM ON THE CROSS WAGGED THEIR HEADS, CURLED THEIR LIPS IN SCORN, TURNED UP THEIR NOSES, AND SARCASTICALLY UTTERED THE WORDS WHICH ARE RECORDED IN THE MEMOIRS OF THE APOSTLES. "HE CALLED HIMSELF THE SON OF GOD; LET HIM COME DOWN FROM THE CROSS AND WALK! LET GOD SAVE HIM!"

ST. JUSTIN MARTYR

GESTAS, THE BAD THIEF

He didn't have to be the Bad Thief.

Two men hung on crosses beside Jesus on Calvary, Dismas and Gestas. One is remembered as the good thief, the other as the bad. But he didn't have to end that way.

Gestas mocked Jesus: "Are you not the Messiah? Save yourself and us!" (Lk 23:39). Maybe his words came from anger, maybe from despair. He was in pain. He was dying. And yet, instead of using his final breaths to pray, he spent them in ridicule and scorn.

We might wonder why. Was Gestas too proud to admit he was wrong? Too hurt, too hardened, to believe mercy was still possible for him?

The sobering truth is this: Gestas had the same chance as Dismas. He was no farther from Jesus. He heard the same silence from Christ when the soldiers mocked him. He saw the same suffering. But while Dismas turned to Jesus, Gestas turned away.

And yet, he didn't have to. He could have chosen differently, right up to that final breath.

How often do we find ourselves in Gestas's place? Wounded, angry, tempted to close our hearts. We stand just as close to Christ as he did, whether we notice him or not. And every moment is another chance. Until the last one.

The story of Gestas isn't just about lost opportunity for conversion; it's about how even the hardest heart still has the freedom to turn to the Lord. Right now, today, we don't have to choose Gestas's bitterness.

Not because we deserve it. Not because we know how to fix everything. But because he is already near. And that nearness means our story isn't finished yet. It's never too late to turn toward mercy.

REFLECT

1. In what ways have you found yourself hardening your heart toward God or others? How does the contrast between Dismas and Gestas help you reflect on your own choices?
2. What does it mean that, even in his last moments, Gestas had the opportunity to turn to Christ? What does his story reveal about the urgency of repentance?

PRAY

MERCIFUL JESUS, I DO NOT WANT TO WASTE THE TIME YOU HAVE GIVEN ME. KEEP ME FROM BITTERNESS, PRIDE, AND DESPAIR. WHEN I AM TEMPTED TO TURN AWAY FROM YOU, SOFTEN MY HEART TO HEAR YOUR VOICE. SAVE ME FROM EVER MOCKING YOU OR LOOKING WITH DISGUST UPON YOUR WAYS. AMEN.

WEEK OF ASH WEDNESDAY

SATURDAY

WHEN YOU FEAR THE DEATH OF YOUR FLESH, YOU OCCASION THE DEATH OF YOUR SOUL. JUST AS MUCH AS IT IS LIFE TO CONFESS CHRIST, IT IS DEATH TO DENY HIM. . . . THE FRAILTY OF PETER HIMSELF ACKNOWLEDGED ITS SIN WHEN HE WITNESSED BY HIS TEARS THE EVIL HE HAD DONE IN DENYING CHRIST.

ST. AUGUSTINE

SIMON PETER

I descended the stone steps under the church in silence, leaving behind the bright Jerusalem afternoon. The air in the lower cistern felt cool and heavy. Tradition holds that this pit, carved into bedrock beneath Caiaphas's house, is where Christ was held after his arrest. Above, centuries before, Simon Peter stood beside a fire, chatting with servants (Jn 18:18).

The walls were close around me, rough and ancient. I stood with my hand on the cold stone. Slowly, I read aloud the words of Psalm 88: "You have put me in the depths of the Pit, in the regions dark and deep . . ." Here, the Lord was alone, awaiting judgment. I let the silence settle after the final line: "You have caused friend and neighbor to shun me; my companions are in darkness" (Ps 88:6, 18).

And that's when I heard it. Clear and sudden, from somewhere up on the hill above: a rooster crowing. Not a recording. Not part of a guided tour. A living, unmistakable sound.

I stood absolutely still, feeling it in my chest. It was like scripture had stepped out of time. I couldn't help but think of Peter—so sure of himself, so ready to stand with Christ, until fear overtook him. He did not want Christ to wash his feet. Three times he denied Christ. The rooster crowed, and he saw himself as he truly was.

In that moment, standing in the pit where Christ was held, I wasn't just remembering Peter's story. I was in it. His weakness was my weakness. His bitter tears could have been mine.

But there was also something else—mercy. Because Peter's story didn't end with failure. It began again in love.

The rooster's crow took on a new meaning for me that day. It could no longer be a cry of shame. It was a summons. A call to return, to begin again with Christ, even from the lowest place.

REFLECT

1. In what ways can moments of failure become a summons rather than a source of shame? How can you cultivate the humility to acknowledge your weakness and the trust to begin again in love?
2. Where in your life do you most need to hear the rooster's crow as a call to return to Christ?

PRAY

LORD JESUS, YOU KNEW PETER'S WEAKNESS AND STILL CALLED HIM YOUR FRIEND. WHEN I FALL, HELP ME TO SEE MY FAILURE NOT AS THE END BUT AS A SUMMONS TO RETURN. LET EVERY REMINDER OF MY WEAKNESS BE AN INVITATION TO TRUST YOUR MERCY MORE DEEPLY. CALL ME BACK, AGAIN AND AGAIN, UNTIL ONE DAY WHEN I AM HOME WITH YOU FOREVER. AMEN.

FIRST WEEK OF LENT

Pontius Pilate and his wife, Claudia Procula

FIRST WEEK OF LENT

SUNDAY

HE JUDGES NOT, AND DO YOU JUDGE? HE SAYS THAT "WHOEVER BELIEVES IN ME MAY NOT REMAIN IN DARKNESS," THAT IS, THAT IF HE IS IN DARKNESS HE MAY NOT REMAIN THAT WAY BUT MAY AMEND HIS ERROR, CORRECT HIS FAULT AND KEEP MY COMMANDMENTS. FOR I HAVE SAID, "I DO NOT DESIRE THE DEATH OF THE WICKED, BUT THEIR CONVERSION."

ST. AMBROSE

REPENTANCE

When we hear the word *repentance*, our minds often go first to sorrow for sin, self-examination, and making amends. All of that is real and necessary. But the saints remind us that at its deepest level, repentance is not just turning *away* from sin—it's turning *toward* God. And to turn toward him means to allow ourselves to be loved by him.

St. Elizabeth of the Trinity, in her last writings, gave this startling counsel to her prioress: "Let yourself be loved more than these." She wrote that Christ's love "can rebuild what you have destroyed" and that he wants to work in us freely, not because we have earned it, but simply because he delights in loving us. Repentance, in her view, is not groveling in shame before a reluctant God—it's opening our hearts to the God who is eager to pour his mercy into them.

Think of the prodigal son. He comes home rehearsing his confession, expecting to be treated as a servant. But before he can finish, his father runs to him, embraces him, and restores him as a son (Lk 15:11–32). That's what repentance looks like in the light of divine love. It's not bargaining with God or earning back his favor—it's collapsing into his arms.

This is hard for us because we are so used to earning. Even our spiritual life can become a subtle contest of self-reliance: *If I pray better, fast harder, serve more, maybe God will be pleased with me again.*

When we truly repent, we begin to see ourselves not as hopeless cases but as beloved children. We realize that God's love is not diminished by our sin, nor is his ability to transform us limited by our weakness. "He will do everything in you," Elizabeth promises, "even though you will have done nothing to attract this grace except that which a creature can do: works of sin and misery. He loves you like that."

And so Lent becomes less about self-condemnation and more about self-surrender. We don't minimize our sin; we bring it into the light where his mercy can reach it. We don't excuse our failures; we hand them over to the one who can rebuild what we have destroyed. Faith in God's love, especially in times of dryness, is one of the purest forms of repentance—it keeps us turned toward him when everything in us wants to turn away.

This Lent, hear Christ's words to you: "Let yourself be loved more than these." Bring him your sins, your regrets, your fears. Let him carry them. Let him carry you. Trust that he will go to the very end to bring you home.

REFLECT

1. When you think of repentance, do you tend to focus more on your own efforts to "make things right" or on God's desire to pour his love into your life? Why? In what ways has pride or shame made it hard for you to receive God's love freely and without condition?
2. St. Elizabeth of the Trinity says that God's love "can rebuild what you have destroyed." What in your life do you most need to bring to him for rebuilding this Lent?
3. How does the parable of the prodigal son challenge your own ideas of what it means to return to God after sin?

PRAY

LORD JESUS, YOU KNOW ME THROUGH AND THROUGH, YET YOU LOVE ME STILL. GIVE ME THE HUMILITY TO BRING YOU MY FAILURES, THE COURAGE TO BELIEVE IN YOUR MERCY, AND THE FAITH TO LET MYSELF BE LOVED. MAY I NEVER TURN AWAY FROM YOUR LOVE BUT INSTEAD REMAIN IN IT ALWAYS. AMEN.

FIRST WEEK OF LENT

MONDAY

REPENTANCE IS JUDGED NOT BY QUANTITY OF TIME, BUT BY DISPOSITION OF THE SOUL. FOR THE NINEVITES DID NOT NEED MANY DAYS TO BLOT OUT THEIR SIN, . . . AND THE ROBBER ALSO DID NOT TAKE A LONG TIME TO EFFECT HIS ENTRANCE INTO PARADISE, BUT IN SUCH A BRIEF MOMENT AS ONE MIGHT OCCUPY IN UTTERING A SINGLE WORD, DID HE WASH OFF ALL THE SINS WHICH HE HAD COMMITTED IN HIS WHOLE LIFE, AND RECEIVED THE PRIZE BESTOWED BY THE DIVINE APPROVAL EVEN BEFORE THE APOSTLES.

ST. JOHN CHRYSOSTOM

DISMAS, THE GOOD THIEF

The gospels tell us nothing about Dismas, the Good Thief, until the final moments of his life. One ancient legend recounts a beautiful possibility worth our meditation: As a young man, Dismas encountered the Holy Family during their flight into Egypt. A bandit, he spared the Child Jesus, moved by something he saw in that innocent face. He could not have known that day that the mercy he showed would one day be returned in abundance.

In the gospels, we meet Dismas on Calvary. Crucified next to Christ, he is given one last chance. And in that moment, surrounded by jeers and suffocating in pain, he speaks perhaps the most important words of his life: "Jesus, remember me when you come into your kingdom" (Lk 23:42).

St. Augustine reflects on this moment, asking, "On what ground was the thief, after receiving praise, deemed worthy to be that same day in Paradise? Because when bound on the cross he confessed Christ, while the disciples doubted concerning him." Dismas believed when belief seemed impossible. His was a conversion measured not in years of penance but in the disposition of a heart finally turned toward God.

St. John Chrysostom puts it even more plainly: "Repentance is judged not by quantity of time, but by disposition of the soul." Dismas had only minutes left. Yet in those minutes, he washed away a lifetime of sin with one sincere act of faith.

This is the hope Lent places before us. It's never too late. Today—whether it's our first Lent as Catholics or our last Lent on this side of eternity, whether we feel near to God or far—is the right day to return. Like Dismas, we don't need a lifetime to be changed. We need one honest prayer: "Jesus, remember me."

And he will.

REFLECT

1. What part of your heart have you held back from God, believing it's too late to change? Bring it to him today in prayer, and ask for the grace to surrender it fully, even if only with the words "Jesus, remember me."
2. Are you willing, like Dismas, to make one sincere act of faith today, even in the midst of pain or doubt?

PRAY

LORD JESUS, REMEMBER ME. IN MY WEAKNESS, REMEMBER ME. IN MY SIN AND IN MY SORROW, REMEMBER ME. YOU DID NOT TURN AWAY FROM DISMAS ON THE CROSS—TURN NOT AWAY FROM ME NOW. AMEN.

FIRST WEEK OF LENT

TUESDAY

PILATE WAS FULL OF ANXIETY . . . AND THOUGHT CAESAR'S RULE WAS ENDANGERED. THEREFORE HE WAS ANXIOUS TO LEARN THE TRUTH IN ORDER TO MEET WHAT HAD BEEN DONE WITH APPROPRIATE RETRIBUTION AND ACQUIT OF BLAME THE OFFICE ENTRUSTED TO HIM BY THE ROMANS.

ST. CYRIL OF ALEXANDRIA

PONTIUS PILATE

Who is this man?

That question lingers in Pontius Pilate's mind, though he would rather be done with Jesus of Nazareth altogether. Pilate is no friend to the local religion; Roman justice is practical, not theological. And yet, as the silent prisoner stands before him, Pilate cannot ignore this question: Who is this man?

"Are you the King of the Jews?" Pilate asks. It's not merely political curiosity; it's something deeper, unsettled. Jesus does not answer as Pilate expects. "My kingdom," Jesus says, "is not from this world." Pilate is caught between cynicism and awe. "What is truth?" he murmurs, revealing both his doubt and his longing (Jn 18:33–38).

And still, the idea gnaws at him. Even as he orders Jesus to be crucified, Pilate writes it plainly: "Jesus of Nazareth, the King of the Jews" (Jn 19:19). The chief priests protest, but Pilate refuses to change it: "What I have written I have written" (Jn 19:22).

Pilate's question echoes through the centuries. We, too, live in a tension between knowing and not knowing. We say that Christ is King, yet we hesitate to let him reign fully in our lives. We call him Lord, yet we wash our hands like Pilate, reluctant to let his kingship overturn our comforts.

Pilate's story warns us of the cost of indecision. Facing Truth himself, Pilate could not bring himself to believe or to submit. He recognized something extraordinary but left it to others to act. And so, the True King was enthroned on a cross, his kingdom proclaimed in mockery—but in truth, for all to see.

Today, Christ still asks each of us the same question Pilate asked him: Are you a king? And we must answer—not with words only but with the shape of our lives.

Who is this man?

He is my King.

REFLECT

1. Read Pilate's encounter with Christ in John 18:24–19:16. What strikes you about Pilate that you have not noticed before?
2. Where in your life are you tempted to "wash your hands" instead of standing for the truth? Identify one such place today and resolve to speak or act with courage, even if it costs you comfort.
3. Do you allow Christ to reign in every part of your life, or do you keep areas under your control? Invite Jesus into one area you've kept off-limits. Ask him to rule there with truth and mercy.

PRAY

LORD JESUS, YOU STOOD SILENT BEFORE PILATE, BUT YOUR SILENCE SPEAKS STILL. YOU ARE TRUTH MADE FLESH, AND YET SO OFTEN I HESITATE TO LET YOU RULE IN ME. FORGIVE ME FOR THE TIMES I HAVE WASHED MY HANDS, CHOOSING COMFORT OVER CONVICTION, COMPROMISE OVER COURAGE. YOU ARE MY KING; REIGN IN MY HEART TODAY. AMEN.

FIRST WEEK OF LENT

WEDNESDAY

THIS DREAM WAS NO SMALL EVENT. IT SHOULD HAVE BEEN ENOUGH TO STOP THEM IN THEIR TRACKS. . . . WHY DIDN'T THE DREAM COME TO PILATE? PERHAPS SHE WAS MORE WORTHY. OR PERHAPS BECAUSE, EVEN IF HE HAD SEEN IT, HE WOULD NOT HAVE EQUALLY BELIEVED OR PERHAPS WOULD NOT HAVE EVEN MENTIONED IT. SO IT WAS PROVIDENTIALLY ARRANGED THAT THE WIFE SHOULD SEE IT, IN ORDER THAT IT MIGHT BECOME MORE COMMONLY KNOWN. AND NOTE THAT SHE DOES NOT ONLY BEHOLD THE DREAM BUT ALSO SUFFERS FROM IT.

ST. JOHN CHRYSOSTOM

CLAUDIA PROCULA, WIFE OF PONTIUS PILATE

Claudia is brief, but her anguish is clear. "Have nothing to do with that innocent man, for today I have suffered a great deal because of a dream about him," she warns her husband, Pontius Pilate (Mt 27:19).

Tradition holds that her dream was no ordinary disturbance of sleep—it was a prophetic warning. Some early Christian writers imagined she glimpsed not just the suffering of Jesus but its eternal ripple: generations reciting, "He was crucified under Pontius Pilate," again and again in churches throughout the world whenever the Nicene Creed is prayed. The dream showed her a judgment far beyond Roman courts: a trial that has lasted through the ages.

Claudia stands before us as a figure of uneasy conscience. She sees the truth from afar, feels its weight in her heart, yet cannot stop what unfolds. Her warning to Pilate is a cry of the heart caught between power and helplessness, between knowing what is right and lacking the strength or power to act decisively. How could he not have felt some sympathy toward her, seeing her suffer because of her dream? How could this not have made his situation even more agonizing?

During Lent, we can see ourselves in Claudia. How often does grace whisper into our lives—through dreams, through conscience, through unexpected moments of clarity? How often do we feel the quiet nudge that warns, "Turn back. Do not go through with this. Let it go"?

Claudia's words are a challenge: Do not ignore the gentle voice of God when it warns or calls. We cannot undo Pilate's choice, but we can make our own.

This Lent, when the path before us seems unclear, may we be ready to listen for God's voice and, in obedience to the quiet pull of conscience, to respond.

REFLECT

1. When has God whispered to your conscience—and did you listen? Recall one such moment. If you ignored his prompting, resolve now to respond differently when he calls again.
2. How can you better recognize and follow the gentle nudges of grace? Today identify one or two obstacles to address in your life so that you can better hear the voice of God.

PRAY

LORD JESUS, YOU SPEAK NOT ONLY IN THUNDER AND FIRE BUT IN QUIET WARNINGS AND WHISPERED DREAMS. HELP ME, LIKE CLAUDIA, TO KNOW THE WEIGHT OF TRUTH—EVEN WHEN I CANNOT FULLY UNDERSTAND IT. GIVE ME A HEART THAT LISTENS, A CONSCIENCE THAT STIRS, AND THE COURAGE TO ACT WHEN YOU CALL. AMEN.

FIRST WEEK OF LENT

THURSDAY

THERE IS A LIKENESS BETWEEN THE NAMES OF BARABBAS AND JESUS THAT IS NOTHING SHORT OF A TRUE MYSTERY. BARABBAS IS APPOINTED FOR MAKING SEDITION AND WARS AND MURDERS IN THE SOULS OF PEOPLE, BUT JESUS IS APPOINTED FOR ALL GOOD THINGS AS THE SON OF GOD AND PEACE AND WORD AND WISDOM. . . . WHOEVER, THEREFORE, DOES EVIL THINGS IN HIS BODY FREES BARABBAS AND BINDS CHRIST. BUT WHOEVER DOES GOOD THINGS FREES CHRIST AND BINDS BARABBAS.

ORIGEN

BARABBAS, THE PRISONER

Pilate stands before the crowd and offers a choice: Jesus of Nazareth or Barabbas (Mt 27:17).

It is a grotesque parody of justice. Barabbas was no petty thief. The gospels describe him as a revolutionary, an insurrectionist, a man guilty of murder during an uprising. He was a political criminal, a rebel against Roman authority, likely the sort of figure many in the crowd admired in secret. In their eyes, he fought for freedom. Jesus, by contrast, stood silent, bloodied, crowned with thorns. His kingdom was not of this world.

But Pilate's offer is chilling in its clarity: Choose your savior. The man of violence, or the man of peace. The man who would kill for his cause, or the one who would lay down his life for his friends.

Barabbas is chosen. He is released. Barabbas offered no apology. He showed no change of heart. As far as we know, he didn't even look back.

Tertullian, one of the Church Fathers, saw the drama clearly: "Barabbas, the most abandoned criminal, is released, as if he were the innocent man; while the most righteous Christ is delivered to be put to death, as if he were the murderer." Barabbas goes free. Jesus is bound.

Even his name underscores the choice at hand: *Bar-Abbas*, "son of the father." His sonship is deceptive. He is a rebel and a murderer, one who sought freedom through violence and bloodshed.

Jesus, the true Son of the eternal Father, came to bring a different kind of liberation—not from Roman rule but from sin and death itself. Barabbas took life in pursuit of his cause; Jesus gave his own life for the sake of others.

The crowd chooses the counterfeit son, the one who mirrors their worldly expectations. Yet in the mystery of grace, the true

Son of the Father goes to the Cross in Barabbas's place—and in ours—offering mercy not to the deserving but to the condemned.

We are Barabbas: sons and daughters of the Father, standing free because of Christ's sacrifice.

REFLECT

1. Where in your life are you tempted to choose the counterfeit over the true Son—security, success, control—instead of surrendering to Christ's peace and mercy? Ask the Lord to help you recognize the false saviors you may follow.
2. Barabbas disappears from the gospels without a word. How will you respond differently to the mercy you've received? What is one concrete action you can take this Lent to live as a child of the Father, redeemed by the Son?

PRAY

LORD JESUS, YOU STOOD SILENT WHILE THE GUILTY WENT FREE. IN BARABBAS, I SEE MYSELF—UNWORTHY, YET RELEASED. I DID NOT EARN YOUR MERCY. I DID NOT ASK FOR IT. YET STILL, YOU CHOSE THE CROSS IN MY PLACE. HELP ME REJECT EVERY FALSE SAVIOR AND WORLDLY HOPE. BREAK THE CHAINS OF PRIDE, ANGER, AND SELF-RELIANCE IN ME. TEACH ME TO RECEIVE YOUR GIFT OF FREEDOM WITH HUMILITY. AMEN.

FIRST WEEK OF LENT

FRIDAY

CAIAPHAS MAKES A TRUE STATEMENT, HIS WORDS BEING VERIFIED NOT BY THE PERVERSITY OF THE PEOPLE BUT BY THE POWER AND WISDOM OF GOD. . . . FOR HE PROCLAIMS BEFOREHAND OF WHAT GOOD THINGS THE DEATH OF THE CHRIST WOULD BECOME THE SOURCE. HE SPEAKS OF WHAT HE DOES NOT UNDERSTAND, GLORIFYING GOD . . . UNDER CONSTRAINT, SINCE HE WAS HOLDING THE PREROGATIVE OF THE PRIESTLY ORDER. THE PROPHECY WAS GIVEN, AS IT WERE, NOT TO HIM PERSONALLY BUT TO THE OUTWARD REPRESENTATIVE OF THE PRIESTHOOD.

ST. CYRIL OF ALEXANDRIA

CAIAPHAS, THE HIGH PRIEST

Joseph ben Caiaphas was the high priest; that is, he was Israel's spiritual leader, entrusted with offering sacrifice on behalf of the people. He knew the law. He knew the scriptures. He held the highest religious office in the land. And it was Caiaphas, ironically, who declared, "It is better for you to have one man die for the people than to have the whole nation destroyed" (Jn 11:50).

His words sound shrewd. They sound like the judgment of a man who has borne responsibility for his people. These are the carefully chosen words of a seasoned politician. But the Gospel of John reveals something deeper: Caiaphas "did not say this on his own" but unknowingly spoke a divine prophecy (Jn 11:51).

This is the mystery: Caiaphas speaks the truth but does not know it. The high priest speaks a prophecy about the true High Priest—but he does not believe it. Standing before the incarnate Son of God, Caiaphas chooses to defend the fragile status quo. He fears Rome more than he fears the Lord. He prefers the illusion of control to the risk of conversion.

When Jesus is questioned before the Sanhedrin, Caiaphas rises and puts Jesus under oath: "Tell us if you are the Messiah, the Son of God." Jesus answers with unflinching authority: "You have said so. But I tell you, from now on you will see the Son of Man seated at the right hand of Power and coming on the clouds of heaven" (Mt 26:63–64).

With that, Caiaphas tears his garments. He accuses Jesus of blasphemy. The verdict is death.

Caiaphas is a tragic figure, a warning for us all. He is not a villain in the way we often imagine one—twisting a mustache, scheming in shadows, delighting in malice. No, Caiaphas is far more unsettling than that. He is not a caricature of evil; he is a religious man. A respected man. A man vested with sacred authority. He leads the prayers of the people. He offers sacrifice in the Temple. He guards the holy traditions passed down through the generations.

And that is what makes his failure so sobering.

Caiaphas does not fail because he does not want to love God. He fails because he does not recognize God standing before him.

REFLECT

1. Caiaphas was a religious leader who missed the presence of God. How do routines or leadership roles sometimes make it harder to remain spiritually open and humble?
2. What does Caiaphas's story teach you about the danger of mistaking human authority or tradition for God's will? How can you keep discerning God's voice, even amid familiarity and comfort?

PRAY

LORD JESUS, FORGIVE ME FOR THE TIMES I HAVE RESISTED YOU, WHEN I HAVE CLUNG TO COMFORT INSTEAD OF CONVERSION, TO CONTROL INSTEAD OF SURRENDER. KEEP MY HEART SOFT. DO NOT LET ME BECOME HARDENED BY PRIDE OR FEAR, EVEN IN THE NAME OF RELIGION. LET YOUR VOICE SPEAK LOUDER THAN MY DESIRE FOR APPROVAL OR POWER. HELP ME TO RECOGNIZE YOU WHEN YOU COME—EVEN IF YOU COME IN WAYS I DO NOT EXPECT. AMEN.

FIRST WEEK OF LENT

SATURDAY

IS THIS THE CROWD WHO WOULD APPLAUD HIS CRUCIFIXION? HOW WAS THEIR HATRED EARNED FROM HIS GRACE? . . . THEY ARE CALLING UPON THE SON OF DAVID. THEY ARE CELEBRATING THE INHERITANCE OF THE ETERNAL KINGDOM. THEY ARE PROCLAIMING BLESSING IN THE NAME OF THE LORD. SOON THEIR SHOUTING OF "CRUCIFY HIM!" WOULD BE BLASPHEMY.

ST. HILARY OF POITIERS

THE CROWD

Jesus was no stranger to crowds.

During the Lord's public ministry, they came from near and far to hear him speak or in hopes of witnessing a miracle. After the feeding of the five thousand, a crowd even tried to make him king (Jn 6:14–15). But when Jesus challenged them to seek not perishable bread but the true bread from heaven, many walked away.

Again and again, crowds came to see Jesus, but they did not truly understand him.

Only days separate the two cries: "Hosanna to the Son of David!" and "Crucify him!"

When Jesus entered Jerusalem, the crowds laid palm branches before him (Jn 12:13). They welcomed him as king, as deliverer. But by the end of the week, that same crowd gathered in the courtyard before Pilate, shouting for his death.

How did their hearts turn so quickly?

The crowd in Jerusalem wasn't entirely different from us. Their hopes were high. They expected Jesus to act according to their desires—to overthrow Roman rule, to restore Israel's glory, to solve their problems as they saw them.

When Jesus refused to be that kind of king, disappointment crept in. By Friday, stirred by fear and pressure from the leaders, the same people who once cheered him now condemned him. "Crucify him!" they shouted, caught up in the momentum of the crowd (Jn 19:15).

Lent invites us to see ourselves in the crowd. It is easy to follow Christ when things are going as we expect, when it costs us little. It is harder to remain faithful when Christ's path leads to the cross, when his ways seem slow or confusing or lonely or difficult. After all, the voices of the crowd echo not just in history but in the hidden places of our own hearts.

REFLECT

1. What expectations do you place on Jesus that might lead you to disappointment or frustration when he does not act as you wish? Do you follow him for who he is or for what you hope he will do for you?
2. Are you ever swayed by the voices around you —culture, peers, pressures—rather than by the truth of Christ? In what areas of your life are you most susceptible to going along with the crowd?
3. When have you praised God publicly but denied him in private—through silence, compromise, or sin? What does that reveal about the strength of your commitment?

PRAY

LORD JESUS, YOU WERE WELCOMED WITH CHEERS AND REJECTED WITH CRIES OF HATRED. YOU LOVED THE CROWD, EVEN WHEN THEY TURNED ON YOU. YOU LOVE ME STILL, EVEN WHEN I DO THE SAME. MAY MY HEART NEVER ECHO "CRUCIFY HIM." INSTEAD, LET IT ALWAYS AND EVERYWHERE WHISPER, "HOSANNA. SAVE ME, LORD." AMEN.

SECOND WEEK OF LENT

The Blessed Virgin Mary and John, the Beloved Disciple

SECOND WEEK OF LENT

SUNDAY

THERE IS A BREADTH OF PATIENCE IN OUR LORD'S PARABLES, THE PATIENCE OF THE SHEPHERD THAT MAKES HIM SEEK AND FIND THE STRAYING SHEEP. IMPATIENCE WOULD READILY TAKE NO ACCOUNT OF A SINGLE SHEEP, BUT PATIENCE UNDERTAKES THE WEARISOME SEARCH. HE CARRIES IT ON HIS SHOULDERS AS A PATIENT BEARER OF A FORSAKEN SINNER. . . . REPENTANCE IS NOT WASTED BECAUSE IT MEETS UP WITH PATIENCE!

TERTULLIAN

TRUST

Lent has a way of surfacing our fears. Sometimes it's in fasting—when hunger reminds us how much we rely on comfort. Sometimes it's in prayer—when silence forces us to face our restlessness. Sometimes it's in almsgiving—when generosity feels like letting go of what we might "need later."

Beneath those moments often lies a deeper question: *Do I really trust God?*

St. Francis de Sales gives us a tender, almost childlike answer. He tells us that the measure of God's providence we experience in our lives depends on the measure of trust we place in him. In other words, God is not stingy—he's always giving—but our fearful hearts can close themselves off from receiving.

Francis urges us not to "anticipate the unpleasant events of this life by apprehension." How much time do we spend worrying about what might happen tomorrow or what we'll do if the worst comes? We rehearse disasters in our mind like stage plays, forgetting that the same Father who has cared for us until now will care for us then.

Either he will keep evil from us, Francis says, or he will give us the courage and strength to bear it. The God who led Israel through the wilderness, who fed Elijah by the brook, who calmed the storm with a word—this same God holds the hours ahead.

Lent asks us to take Jesus at his word when he says, "Do not worry about tomorrow" (Mt 6:34). That's not naivete—it's faith. We can let go of what we cannot control because we belong to him. And belonging to him means we're never alone.

Francis paints a beautiful picture of a child in the arms of a father. Children don't strategize how they'll find food or protect themselves from harm—they simply rest in the one who loves them. "What does a child in the arms of such a Father have to fear?"

The truth is that trust grows best when we practice it in the small things. We can't leap into heroic surrender without first handing over today's minor irritations and anxieties: a difficult conversation, an unexpected delay, the ache of a disappointment. Each time we choose to trust, we loosen fear's grip on our heart and strengthen the muscles of faith.

During Lent, we remember that our lives are held in the hands that were pierced for us. If God has already given us his Son, how will he not also give us everything we truly need (see Romans 8:32)? This is not pretending the cross won't come. It is knowing that when it does, we will find Christ already there, carrying it with us. And on the far side of that trust is the joy of Easter—the unshakable happiness of a child in the Father's embrace.

REFLECT

1. When you face uncertainty or fear about the future, do you tend to "anticipate the unpleasant" in your mind? How does this affect your ability to trust God's providence in the present moment?
2. Looking back over your life, where can you clearly see that God has cared for you—protecting you, guiding you, or giving you the strength to endure?
3. Are there small, everyday worries you can begin surrendering to God as a way to grow in trust before the bigger trials come?

PRAY

LORD, MY FATHER AND MY REFUGE, I PLACE MYSELF IN YOUR HANDS TODAY. HELP ME TO REST IN YOU AS A CHILD RESTS IN A FATHER'S ARMS, CONFIDENT THAT YOU WILL GIVE ME WHATEVER I TRULY NEED. MAY MY TRUST IN YOUR PROVIDENCE GROW DEEPER THIS LENT UNTIL I CAN SAY WITH ALL MY HEART, "YOU ARE MY GOD, AND I WILL TRUST IN YOU, NOW AND FOREVER." AMEN.

SECOND WEEK OF LENT

MONDAY

SIMEON PROPHESIES ABOUT MARY HERSELF, THAT WHEN STANDING BY THE CROSS AND SEEING WHAT IS BEING DONE AND HEARING THE VOICES, AFTER THE WITNESS OF GABRIEL, AFTER HER SECRET KNOWLEDGE OF THE DIVINE CONCEPTION, AFTER THE GREAT EXHIBITION OF MIRACLES, SHE SHALL FEEL ABOUT HER SOUL A MIGHTY TEMPEST. THE LORD WAS BOUND TO TASTE OF DEATH FOR EVERY HUMAN BEING.

ST. BASIL THE GREAT

THE BLESSED VIRGIN MARY

From the beginning, Mary stood by Christ.

She stood by him in Bethlehem, cradling the mystery of the Incarnate Word.

She stood by him in Nazareth, quietly watching him grow in wisdom and grace.

She stood by him as he began to teach, as crowds followed and miracles unfolded. She heard his voice, saw his hands heal, and kept all these things in her heart.

St. John tells us, "Standing near the cross of Jesus were his mother . . ." (Jn 19:25). At the end—when the crowds turned, when the disciples fled—she stood by him still.

Mary's life was a continual *fiat*—a yes spoken not only with her lips but with her presence.

When the prophet Simeon foretold that a sword would pierce her soul, Mary did not withdraw. When Jesus disappeared in the Temple, she searched with a mother's anxious heart—and kept pondering. When the time had come, she prompted him to begin his public ministry at Cana. Her discipleship was not built on comfort, certainty, or control. It was built on trust—quiet, confident, and enduring.

She is every mother who has stood helpless beside the suffering of her child. She is the mother who waits outside the prison walls. She is the mother of the addict, the wayward, the lost. She is the mother at the hospital bed, shaken with sorrow and tears.

Mary stood by—and still she stands. For all who grieve, for all who remain in love when love costs everything, she is there. At the foot of the Cross, her fiat becomes a beacon. She teaches us that to stand by Christ is also to stand by all who suffer, to love when nothing makes sense, and to remain, even when the only word left is *why*.

REFLECT

1. In what ways can you make your yes to God more than words—expressing it through consistent presence and action?
2. When have you stood beside someone in his or her suffering, and what did you learn from that experience? How might Mary's example lead you to see the suffering of others as an opportunity to stand by Christ himself?
3. What "why" questions are you carrying in your own life, and how can you bring them to the foot of the Cross with Mary?

PRAY

MARY, MOTHER OF SORROWS, YOU STOOD BY YOUR SON IN HIS HOUR OF GREATEST SUFFERING. TEACH ME TO STAND FIRM IN FAITH AND LOVE, EVEN WHEN THE CROSS SEEMS UNBEARABLE. STAY WITH ME SO THAT I MAY STAY WITH HIM. AMEN.

SECOND WEEK OF LENT

TUESDAY

HE IS SAID TO HAVE BEEN THE LAST ONE WHO EMBARKED ON WRITING A GOSPEL. CHRIST HAD MOVED AND ROUSED HIM TO THE WORK, WHICH IS WHY HE CONTINUALLY SETS FORTH HIS LOVE, ALLUDING TO THE CAUSE BY WHICH HE WAS IMPELLED TO WRITE. THEREFORE HE ALSO CONTINUALLY MAKES MENTION OF IT, TO MAKE HIS RECORD TRUSTWORTHY AND TO SHOW THAT HE CAME TO THIS WORK MOTIVATED BY THAT LOVE.

ST. JOHN CHRYSOSTOM

JOHN, THE BELOVED DISCIPLE

Among the Twelve, there was a disciple known simply as "the one whom Jesus loved." At the Last Supper, he reclined close to Jesus, resting on his chest (Jn 13:23). It is a moment of profound intimacy—the closeness of a friend who knows he is loved and who is unafraid to draw near.

This beloved disciple does not speak many words in the Passion narrative. But his actions speak volumes. While others flee, he remains. He is there in Gethsemane. He follows Jesus to the high priest's courtyard. And finally, at the foot of the Cross, he stands beside the Blessed Mother—silent, steady, faithful.

Whereas Peter swore he would never deny Jesus but then did, the beloved disciple never made such promises. He is a loyal friend.

There is a powerful connection between the disciple who rests on Jesus's heart and the one who reveals his loyalty at the foot of the Cross. The one who draws near in love is also the one who can remain in suffering. The one who listens deeply to the heart of Christ is the one made strong enough to follow him to Calvary.

Because he stayed, the beloved disciple became a privileged witness—leaning on the heart of Jesus, he later revealed that heart to the world. "He who saw this has testified," he writes, so that we, too, might believe (Jn 19:35).

During Lent, we are invited to be that disciple. To draw near to Jesus in prayer. To rest on his heart in the quiet moments of Eucharistic Adoration or silent reflection. And then, having known his love, to follow him through the trial, the darkness, the Cross.

The beloved disciple shows us that true discipleship is not about bold declarations or perfect courage but about intimacy with Christ that bears fruit in enduring fidelity. He teaches us that love—against every fear and misunderstanding—is what gives us strength to remain.

REFLECT

1. Have you made space in your life to "rest on the heart of Jesus" through Eucharistic Adoration, scripture, or silent prayer? Do you rely on the love of Christ to sustain your prayer, or are you looking to your own efforts?
2. What can you learn from John's closeness to Jesus at the Last Supper about the connection between intimacy with Christ and courage in trials?

PRAY

LORD JESUS, YOU DREW THE BELOVED DISCIPLE NEAR TO YOUR HEART. DRAW ME CLOSE TO YOU IN PRAYER SO THAT MY LOVE FOR YOU MAY DEEPEN AND STEADY ME WHEN TRIALS COME. GIVE ME THE COURAGE TO REMAIN WITH YOU AT THE CROSS, AND THE TENDERNESS TO CARE FOR THOSE YOU PLACE IN MY LIFE AS JOHN CARED FOR YOUR MOTHER. LET MY FIDELITY BE ROOTED NOT IN MY OWN STRENGTH BUT IN THE LOVE I HAVE FOUND IN YOU. AMEN.

SECOND WEEK OF LENT

WEDNESDAY

"HIS SISTERS SENT A MESSAGE TO JESUS SAYING, LORD, THE FRIEND WHOM YOU LOVE IS SICK" (JN 11:3). BY THESE WORDS THEY APPEAL TO HIS AFFECTION, THEY LAY CLAIM TO HIS FRIENDSHIP, THEY CALL ON HIS LOVE, URGING THEIR FAMILIAR RELATIONSHIP WITH HIM TO PERSUADE HIM TO RELIEVE THEIR DISTRESS. BUT FOR CHRIST IT WAS MORE IMPORTANT TO CONQUER DEATH THAN TO CURE DISEASE. HE SHOWED HIS LOVE FOR HIS FRIEND NOT BY HEALING HIM BUT BY CALLING HIM BACK FROM THE GRAVE. INSTEAD OF A REMEDY FOR HIS ILLNESS, HE OFFERED HIM THE GLORY OF RISING FROM THE DEAD.

ST. PETER CHRYSOLOGUS

LAZARUS OF BETHANY

Six days before Passover, Jesus goes to Bethany (Jn 12:1).

It is not a random stop. He was not simply returning to a village he loved one last time. It is a deliberate visit to the man he once called out of the tomb. To the man who had been dead four days. To Lazarus, the friend whose breath bears witness to the awesome power of God.

He shares a meal with him in his home. Lazarus reclines with him at table. Lazarus's sisters, of course, are present too. Martha serves, as she always does. Mary breaks open a jar of costly perfume and anoints his feet with a love so extravagant that it scandalizes Judas.

But Lazarus anchors the scene. He once walked out of death. Lazarus heard the voice of the Son of God call to him in his grave, "Come out" (Jn 11:43). He is, quite literally, a living sign of what Jesus has come to accomplish. His presence at table is a declaration for any with eyes to see: Love is stronger than death.

And so Jesus lingers in Bethany—before he enters Jerusalem, before the shouts of "Hosanna" turn to cries of "Crucify him!"—pausing in the company of this beloved household. "He went to Jerusalem so that he might die there, but to Bethany so that the raising up of Lazarus might be imprinted more deeply on the memory of all," writes St. Bede. On the way to his suffering and death, Our Lord rests with those who have already seen a glimpse of the Resurrection.

We don't know what words Jesus and Lazarus exchanged that evening. But perhaps they didn't need many. Perhaps the bond of suffering and mercy was enough. In a word, it was the bond of friendship.

There must have been laughter. And tears.

REFLECT

1. Lazarus heard the voice of Christ calling him from the tomb. What are the "tombs" in your own life—places of sin, fear, or despair—where you need to hear Christ speak life again?
2. Lazarus's very presence was a testimony to Jesus's victory over death. How does your life bear witness to his saving power? Do you share those moments with others so that they might believe?
3. Our Lord lingered with Lazarus, Mary, and Martha before going to Jerusalem. Where in your life do you make room for your friendship with Christ before facing trials?

PRAY

LORD JESUS, YOU CALLED LAZARUS FROM THE GRAVE AND RESTORED HIM TO LIFE. CALL ME OUT OF THE PLACES WHERE I HAVE BEEN BOUND BY FEAR, SHAME, OR HOPELESSNESS, AND SET ME FREE TO LIVE FULLY IN YOUR LOVE. HELP ME TO BE A LIVING WITNESS, LIKE LAZARUS, WHOSE VERY LIFE TELLS THE STORY OF WHAT YOU HAVE DONE. AMEN.

SECOND WEEK OF LENT

THURSDAY

MARY STANDS FOR EVE, AND JOSEPH STANDS FOR ANOTHER JOSEPH. HE WHO ASKED FOR HIS CORPSE WAS ALSO NAMED JOSEPH. THE EARLIER JOSEPH WAS A RIGHTEOUS MAN WHO DID NOT DENOUNCE MARY PUBLICLY. THE OTHER ONE WAS ALSO A RIGHTEOUS MAN BECAUSE HE DID NOT CONSENT TO THE DETRACTORS. . . . THIS NAME RECEIVES THE FULL REWARD FOR SERVING HIM AT HIS BIRTH IN THE CAVE AND FOR HAVING SERVED HIS CORPSE AT THE TOMB.

ST. EPHREM THE SYRIAN

JOSEPH OF ARIMATHEA

The sky darkened. The earth shook. The disciples had scattered. Christ had breathed his last. The crowds had vanished, and only a few soldiers kept watch at Golgotha.

But then, one man stepped forward.

Joseph of Arimathea, a respected member of the Sanhedrin, a man of rank and reputation, did what none of the Twelve dared to do. He went to Pilate and asked for the body of Jesus (Mk 15:43).

This was no small gesture. Jesus had been condemned as a criminal. His execution was public. To ask for his body was to align himself with the condemned, to risk his name, his status, even his safety. But Joseph did it anyway. He asked for the body of the Lord.

What changed?

Perhaps it was the way Jesus died—with mercy on his lips. Perhaps it was the earthquake, the torn veil, or simply the quiet movement of grace. But something in Joseph could no longer hold back.

He wrapped the body in clean linen. He laid it in a new tomb, carved in stone—a place Joseph had prepared for himself. In this, he fulfilled the words of the prophet: "They made his grave with the wicked and his tomb with the rich" (Is 53:9).

Christ, who had no place to lay his head, now rested in the tomb of a disciple. Not buried in shame, but buried in dignity. Not tossed aside, but reverently entombed.

Remember another Joseph—a just man who, years before, had taken the infant Jesus into his arms, helped his mother to wrap him in swaddling clothes, and laid him in a manger. That first Joseph guarded the Lord's body at the beginning of his earthly life. This second Joseph does so at its end.

The gospels give us no words from Joseph of Arimathea. Only this one, great act. But what it reveals is enough: a man transformed by the Cross. A man who overcame fear. A man who honored the Body of Christ when others turned away.

REFLECT

1. Joseph gave the Lord a tomb he had prepared for himself. What resources, possessions, or opportunities are you holding back from offering to Christ?
2. What does Joseph's boldness after Christ's death teach you about acting with love and faith even when hope feels far away? How might the Lord be calling you to step out of secrecy into open discipleship today?

PRAY

LORD JESUS, JOSEPH OF ARIMATHEA HONORED YOU WHEN IT COST HIM HIS SAFETY, HIS REPUTATION, AND HIS COMFORT. GIVE ME THE COURAGE TO SERVE YOU WITHOUT RESERVE. WHEN OTHERS TURN AWAY, LET ME STEP FORWARD. MAY I OFFER YOU NOT ONLY MY RESOURCES BUT ALSO MY HEART, MAKING SPACE FOR YOU, AS JOSEPH MADE SPACE FOR YOU IN HIS OWN TOMB. AMEN.

SECOND WEEK OF LENT

FRIDAY

FOR NICODEMUS HAD AT FIRST COME TO JESUS BY NIGHT, AS RECORDED BY THIS SAME JOHN IN THE EARLIER PORTIONS OF HIS GOSPEL. BY THE STATEMENT GIVEN US HERE . . . WE ARE TO UNDERSTAND THAT NICODEMUS CAME TO JESUS, NOT THEN ONLY, BUT THEN FOR THE FIRST TIME; AND THAT HE WAS A REGULAR COMER AFTERWARDS, IN ORDER BY HEARING TO BECOME A DISCIPLE.

ST. AUGUSTINE

NICODEMUS, THE PHARISEE

Nicodemus went to see Jesus at night (Jn 3:2).

He was a Pharisee, a respected teacher of Israel, a man of knowledge and reputation. And yet, something in him stirred—some quiet hunger, some restless longing—that led him to seek Jesus in secret. He came under the cover of darkness, when no one would see, when his questions could be safely whispered.

"Rabbi," he said, "we know that you are a teacher who has come from God" (Jn 3:2).

But Jesus did not offer safe answers. He spoke instead of a new birth, a life in the Spirit, a truth that could not be managed or controlled. He told Nicodemus, "You must be born from above" (Jn 3:7). He spoke of the wind that blows where it wills, of the Son of Man lifted up, of a love that saves the world but demands our whole heart in return.

Nicodemus was puzzled. "How can these things be?" he asked (Jn 3:9).

And then he disappears into the darkness. For a time, we hear no more of him.

But later—when the Son of Man has indeed been lifted up on the Cross—Nicodemus returns. Not with more questions, but with action. When Jesus has died, Nicodemus joins Joseph of Arimathea to bury the Lord. He brings a mixture of myrrh and aloes—about a hundred pounds. Not a symbolic gesture. A royal one. Costly. Public. Unmistakable.

Nicodemus takes the Savior's lifeless body into his own hands. With reverence, he anoints the Lord's mangled flesh. He presses spices into linen and wraps his wounded limbs. His hands move with quiet love, performing an act that only the deepest devotion would dare. He prepares Jesus for the tomb as his King.

He who once came by night has stepped into the light.

REFLECT

1. Nicodemus first came to Jesus in secrecy, then later honored him openly. Where in your life are you still living your faith "by night," afraid to be known as a disciple? What would it look like for you to bring you discipleship fully into the light?
2. Nicodemus gave Christ a burial fit for a king. How do you show reverence for his Body—in the Eucharist and in the suffering members of his Church?

PRAY

LORD JESUS, YOU DREW NICODEMUS FROM THE SHADOWS INTO THE LIGHT OF LOVE. DRAW ME OUT OF FEAR AND INTO THE COURAGE TO LIVE AS YOUR DISCIPLE IN THE OPEN. TEACH ME TO SERVE YOUR BODY, THE EUCHARIST, THE CHURCH, AND THE POOR, WITH REVERENCE AND TENDERNESS, KNOWING THAT IN SERVING THEM, I SERVE YOU. AMEN.

SECOND WEEK OF LENT

SATURDAY

THE SAVIOR DOES NOT INQUIRE, "DO YOU BELIEVE THIS?" IN IGNORANCE AS TO WHETHER MARTHA DID OR DID NOT BELIEVE WHAT WAS SAID. RATHER, HE DID SO IN ORDER THAT WE . . . MIGHT LEARN FROM HER ANSWER WHAT HER DISPOSITION WAS. BUT ANOTHER WILL SAY THAT IT IS NOT A QUESTION BUT A STATEMENT: "YOU BELIEVE THIS." IN THIS CASE, MARTHA THEN COMPLETES THE SAVIOR'S STATEMENT SAYING, YES, LORD, AND NOT ONLY DO I BELIEVE WHAT YOU NOW SAY, BUT I BELIEVE NOW THAT YOU ARE THE CHRIST, SOMETHING I ALSO BELIEVED BEFORE.

ORIGEN

MARTHA OF BETHANY

Martha was the doer.

When Jesus visited Bethany, Martha welcomed him into the home. Martha busied herself with service, preparing the table, tending to the details of hospitality. And when her brother Lazarus died, it was Martha—again—who rose and went out to meet the Lord.

Martha, carrying all of her sorrow, went to find Jesus. And when she did, she spoke words full of hope: "Lord, if you had been here, my brother would not have died. But even now I know that God will give you whatever you ask of him" (Jn 11:21–22).

These are not the words of a woman resigned to death. They are the words of a woman who dares to believe—even through tears.

Jesus tells her, "Your brother will rise again."

And Martha, ever the faithful daughter of Israel, affirms her belief in the resurrection on the last day. But Jesus calls her further, deeper, into the mystery of his identity: "I am the resurrection and the life."

"Do you believe this?" the Lord asks.

And Martha replies with one of the most extraordinary professions of faith in all the gospels: "Yes, Lord, I believe that you are the Messiah, the Son of God, the one coming into the world" (Jn 11:23–27).

Martha—who is often remembered simply as the one who cooked and served—is revealed here as one of the first to recognize and confess Jesus for who he truly is. And her prayer, her bold petition for her brother, is answered: Jesus raises Lazarus from the dead.

Martha shows us a model of discipleship that is both active and contemplative, practical and believing. She moves quickly to serve, but she also stands still to listen. She speaks frankly to the Lord, and yet surrenders to his will. She suffers loss but holds fast to hope.

REFLECT

1. Martha came to meet Jesus in her grief, speaking honestly of her pain. How open are you in sharing your deepest sorrows and disappointments with the Lord? How can you grow in faith to believe that he is "the Resurrection and the Life" even before you see the outcome of your prayers?
2. How do you balance the active service of Martha with the listening heart of Mary in your discipleship?
3. In what area of your life is Jesus asking you today, "Do you believe this?" How will you respond?

PRAY

LORD JESUS, YOU MET MARTHA IN HER GRIEF AND CALLED HER TO DEEPER TRUST. MEET ME IN MY OWN SORROWS AND STRENGTHEN MY FAITH SO THAT WITH HER I MAY CONFESS, "YES, LORD, I BELIEVE THAT YOU ARE THE MESSIAH, THE SON OF GOD." GIVE ME THE COURAGE TO HOPE IN YOUR PROMISES, EVEN WHEN ALL SEEMS LOST. AMEN.

THIRD WEEK OF LENT

The Angel in Gethsemane

THIRD WEEK OF LENT

SUNDAY

THEY CAME AND THEY SEIZED HIM. THEY WOULD DIE A MORE DREADFUL DEATH AS A FRUIT OF THEIR ZEAL. THESE WRETCHES DID NOT UNDERSTAND THE MYSTERY NOR REVERE SUCH COMPASSION OF PIETY, BECAUSE CHRIST DID NOT LET EVEN HIS ENEMIES BE WOUNDED. THEY INFLICTED DEATH ON THE RIGHTEOUS ONE, AND HE HEALED [THEIR] WOUNDS.

ST. AMBROSE

COMPASSION

Malcolm Muggeridge once described what it was like to accompany Mother Teresa on her daily work—visiting the Home for the Dying, the lepers, the abandoned children. He said it came to him in three phases.

The first was horror, mixed with pity—the shock of seeing human suffering so raw and unfiltered. The second was compassion, a simpler, gentler feeling: the desire to relieve the suffering before him.

But then came a third phase—something beyond compassion. He found himself seeing these dying, crippled, and forsaken people not as pitiable or repulsive but as dear and delightful—as though they were cherished friends he had known all his life.

How could this be explained? He writes, "To soothe those battered old heads, to grasp those poor stumps, to take in one's arms those children consigned to dustbins, because it is his head, as they are his stumps and his children, of whom he said that whosoever received one such child in his name received him." For Muggeridge, this was nothing less than the heart of the Christian mystery.

Compassion isn't simply noticing pain—it's entering into it with another person, taking it on yourself in some way. The gospels show us again and again that compassion is not a mere sentiment for Jesus—it is a force that moves him to act. St. Matthew tells us that when Jesus saw the crowds, "he had compassion for them, because they were harassed and helpless, like sheep without a shepherd" (Mt 9:36). He drew closer, taught them, fed them, and healed their sick.

In fact, the deepest moment of compassion in history is the Passion itself. "Surely he has borne our griefs and carried our sorrows," Isaiah prophesied (Is 53:4 NKJV). Lent draws us into that truth: The God who could have remained untouched by our pain instead came down into it, shouldering its full weight.

In our own lives, compassion means listening without rushing to fix someone's pain; quietly standing beside someone in grief when there's nothing to say; or taking on a sacrifice—time, resources, emotional energy—to help another carry his or her cross. Real compassion embraces the stranger as well as the friend, stretching beyond the easy boundaries of our comfortable circle.

Lent is a school for compassion. Our fasting can awaken us to the hunger of others. Our almsgiving can open our eyes to the real needs of our neighbors. Our prayer can deepen our union with Christ, whose Sacred Heart is "moved with compassion" for the lost and hurting.

Because the truth is that we can only stand with others in their suffering if we have first stood with Christ in his. And we can only stand with Christ in his suffering if we are ready to let him stand with us in ours.

REFLECT

1. Have you ever stopped at the first stage Muggeridge described—seeing another's suffering with horror or pity—but pulled back before letting it change you? What keeps you from moving deeper into a compassion that truly enters the other's pain?
2. When you encounter suffering, do you try to keep it at arm's length? What would it look like for you to move closer, as Jesus did, allowing someone's burden to touch your own life?

PRAY

LORD JESUS, YOU DREW NEAR TO THE CROWDS WITH A HEART MOVED TO ACT. YOU TOUCHED THE LEPER, WELCOMED THE OUTCAST, AND CARRIED OUR SORROWS TO THE CROSS. HELP ME TO SEE YOUR FACE IN THOSE WHO SUFFER, TO RECOGNIZE THAT THEIR PAIN IS YOUR PAIN. AMEN.

THIRD WEEK OF LENT

MONDAY

THE CROSS OF CHRIST IS THE TRIUMPH OF VIRTUE AND A TROPHY OF VICTORY. HOW BLESSED IS SIMON, WHO DESERVED TO BE THE FIRST TO BEAR SO GREAT A SIGN OF VICTORY! HE WAS COMPELLED TO CARRY THE CROSS BEFORE THE LORD BECAUSE THE LORD WANTED TO DEMONSTRATE HIS CROSS TO BE A SINGULAR GRACE OF THAT HEAVENLY MYSTERY WHICH IS HIMSELF: GOD AND MAN, LOGOS AND FLESH, SON OF GOD AND SON OF MAN. HE WAS CRUCIFIED AS MAN BUT TRIUMPHED AS GOD IN THE MYSTERY OF THE CROSS.

ST. CHROMATIUS

SIMON OF CYRENE

The road to Calvary is long, and the prisoner is growing weak. Beaten, bloodied, and bowed low, Jesus stumbles under the weight of the Cross. The soldiers grow impatient. The Pharisees want the spectacle to continue, but not at this pace. Time must not be lost; the execution must go on.

And so they look around.

They see a man from Cyrene, a stranger in the crowd. He is strong and from the country. Perhaps he was a farmer, perhaps a merchant. We are told his name: Simon. We are told he is the father of Alexander and Rufus (Mk 15:21)—a sign, perhaps, that he was known in the early Church. Or that his sons were. Maybe they were the first beneficiaries of their father's loving service? Converts in the first days of the Church?

Simon does not volunteer. He does not step forward in compassion. He tries, it seems, to just pass by. But he is seized; he is forced to carry the Lord's Cross.

One moment, he is just a passerby. The next, his shoulder is beneath the weight of the wood, carrying a burden that is not his own.

And yet—what grace!

Simon walks with God in the flesh, though he may not know who he is. He feels the splintered beam press against his skin. He hears the heavy breathing of the Man beside him. And he keeps walking.

But why is Simon so well known to each of us if he didn't freely choose to help Jesus?

Because Simon stands for each of us.

At some point, we, too, are pressed into service. We are forced to bear a cross we did not choose—a diagnosis, a betrayal, a grief, a burden we cannot understand. It comes unbidden. It interrupts our plans. It shames our pride. Remember the words of the Lord:

"Whoever does not carry the cross and follow me cannot be my disciple" (Lk 14:27).

And yet—what grace.

In that moment, Christ draws near. We carry the Cross, yes—but not alone. We walk beside the one who bore it first. The one whose strength sanctifies ours. The one who, by sharing his suffering, transforms it into love.

REFLECT

1. Simon did not choose to carry the Cross, yet God allowed it to become the most significant moment of his life. What burdens have entered your life without your consent—illness, loss, responsibilities—and have you resisted them, resented them, or allowed them to draw you closer to Christ?
2. When you see someone else weighed down by suffering—whether physical, emotional, or spiritual—do you quietly slip away, hoping someone else will help? Or do you see such moments as invitations from God to bear the weight with them?
3. In your prayer and daily living, do you ask God to remove your crosses more often than you ask him for the grace to carry them faithfully? How might your spiritual life change if you asked more for endurance and less for escape?

PRAY

LORD JESUS, YOU LET SIMON WALK BESIDE YOU BENEATH THE WEIGHT OF THE CROSS. YOU LET HIM BE CLOSE TO YOU IN YOUR SUFFERING. LET ME NOT RUN FROM THE CROSSES YOU ALLOW IN MY LIFE. GIVE ME THE GRACE TO CARRY THEM WITH YOU—TO SEE IN THEM NOT ONLY PAIN BUT THE NEARNESS OF YOUR PRESENCE. AMEN.

THIRD WEEK OF LENT

TUESDAY

WHATEVER YOU LOVE IS EITHER THE SAME AS YOURSELF, BELOW YOU OR ABOVE YOU. IF WHAT YOU LOVE IS BENEATH YOU, LOVE IT TO COMFORT IT, CARE FOR IT AND TO USE IT BUT NOT TO CLING TO IT. FOR EXAMPLE, YOU LOVE GOLD. DO NOT BECOME ATTACHED TO THE GOLD, FOR HOW MUCH BETTER ARE YOU THAN GOLD? GOLD, INDEED, IS A SHINING PIECE OF EARTH, WHILE YOU HAVE BEEN MADE IN THE IMAGE OF GOD IN ORDER THAT YOU MAY BE ILLUMINED BY THE LORD.

ST. CAESARIUS OF ARLES

VERONICA, BEARER OF THE TRUE IMAGE

Hear the clamor of the streets in Jerusalem. The jeering crowd presses close. Dust rises around the man condemned to die. Amid the noise and hatred, a woman steps forward. In her name, Veronica, we see the very words vera and icon—"the true icon."

She cannot end his pain. She cannot carry his Cross. But she can love him. She can draw near. With trembling hands, she offers a veil, a small gesture of tenderness in a world that has forgotten mercy. She presses the cloth to his face, and when she lifts it again, his image is there—the imprint of the Crucified.

Veronica stands as a symbol of the Church herself. She shows what it means to draw near to the suffering Christ, to console him by our love. And so it is with every act of compassion we offer in his name: The Lord leaves his image upon us and on those we love.

C. S. Lewis understood this mystery. In his bedroom, he kept a framed copy of a photo of the face of the Shroud of Turin—a gift from a nun—to remind him that Christ's face was not a symbol but a reality, human and near. St. Thérèse of Lisieux expressed her own affection in her devotion to the Holy Face: "My only wealth, Lord! is thy Face; / I ask naught else than this from Thee; / Hid in the secret of that Face, / The more I shall resemble thee!" she prayed.

To gaze upon the face of Christ is to be changed by it. That is the truth hidden in the story of Veronica's veil, in Lewis's photograph, in Thérèse's prayer. Each teaches us that love begins in meeting the eyes of the suffering Lord and letting his mercy mark us.

REFLECT

1. Wiping the face of Christ was a small gesture, but how precious it would have been! Do you believe that no act of mercy is wasted, even when the world sees it as insignificant? What small act of compassion is God asking you to offer today?
2. According to tradition, the veil returned to Veronica with the imprint of Christ's face, a visible reminder that those who draw close to him are changed. What would it mean for you to live in such a way that Christ's likeness is visible in your words, choices, and relationships?

PRAY

LORD JESUS, LET ME NOT TURN AWAY FROM YOUR HOLY FACE. IN THE DUST AND NOISE OF THIS WORLD, TEACH ME TO DRAW NEAR TO YOU WITH LOVE. PRESS THE IMAGE OF YOUR MERCY UPON MY HEART SO THAT I MAY BEAR IT TO OTHERS, A LIVING REFLECTION OF YOUR COMPASSION, A TRACE OF YOU IN EVERY PLACE I GO. AMEN.

THIRD WEEK OF LENT

WEDNESDAY

THE PATIENCE OF THE LORD WAS WOUNDED IN THE WOUND OF MALCHUS. AND SO, TOO, HE CURSED FOR THE TIME TO COME THE WORKS OF THE SWORD. AND, BY THE RESTORATION OF HEALTH, MADE SATISFACTION TO HIM WHOM HIMSELF HAD NOT HURT, THROUGH PATIENCE, THE MOTHER OF MERCY.

TERTULLIAN

MALCHUS, SERVANT OF THE HIGH PRIEST

He came with a sword.

Even if he did not brandish one in his hand, he carried a sword in his purpose. Malchus, the servant of the high priest, was part of the crowd sent to arrest Jesus in Gethsemane. It was night, the hour of betrayal. Torches flickered. Tension hung thick in the garden air. And suddenly, chaos broke loose.

One of the disciples, full of fear and zeal, lashed out with a blade—Peter, defending the Lord. But in his rush to fight, he struck not a soldier, not a threat, but a servant (Jn 18:10–11).

The sword slashed through flesh. Blood spilled. Malchus fell back, clutching the side of his head. Pain. Confusion. A fight.

Even in the middle of betrayal—when loyalty has shattered and love has turned to fear—Jesus does not pull away. He does not withhold his hand. In Gethsemane, surrounded by those who came to destroy him, Jesus still notices the one who is hurt. Even as the mob encircles him. Even as the Passion begins. He touches the servant's wounded ear. And heals him (Lk 22:51).

What must that moment have been like? "The clay recognizes its maker, and the flesh follows the hand of the Lord who formed it," writes St. Ambrose, "for the creator repairs his work as he wishes." The last miracle before the Cross—offered not to a disciple, not to a believer, but to one of the very men who had come to bind him.

Malchus came to seize Christ, and instead was touched by mercy.

Our Lord healed Malchus with a touch. He did not wait for repentance, or a confession of faith. He simply responded to pain with mercy.

And so he does with us. He meets our wounds with love. Even in the middle of betrayal. Even when the night seems darkest.

REFLECT

1. The healing of Malchus is the last miracle before the Cross. What does this teach you about the heart of Christ in the face of betrayal and violence? How can you imitate that heart in your own moments of conflict?
2. Peter's sword was meant to defend Jesus, yet it caused harm. Have you ever acted in zeal for God but in a way that wounded others?

PRAY

LORD JESUS, IN THE HOUR OF YOUR BETRAYAL, YOU HEALED THE ONE WHO CAME TO BIND YOU. YOU REACHED OUT TO AN ENEMY AND RESTORED WHAT VIOLENCE HAD TAKEN AWAY. HEAL THE WOUNDS IN MY OWN HEART, AND GIVE ME THE GRACE TO BE AN INSTRUMENT OF PEACE. WHEN I AM TEMPTED TO STRIKE BACK, TEACH ME INSTEAD TO REACH OUT WITH MERCY. LET MY LIFE BEAR WITNESS THAT YOUR LOVE IS STRONGER THAN HATE. AMEN.

THIRD WEEK OF LENT

THURSDAY

THE LORD OVER DEATH SET OUT TO ABOLISH DEATH. BEING LORD, HE ACCOMPLISHED HIS AIM. WE THEREFORE HAVE PASSED FROM DEATH TO LIFE. . . . THAT IS THE REASON OUR SAVIOR RESTRAINED THE WOMEN FROM WEEPING WHEN HE WAS BEING LED TO DEATH. HE SAID, "DO NOT WEEP FOR ME." HE WISHED TO SHOW THAT HIS DEATH WAS NOT AN EVENT FOR US TO MOURN ABOUT BUT RATHER TO BE JOYFUL ABOUT, SINCE HE WHO DIED FOR US IS ALIVE! HE WAS NOT CREATED FROM NOTHING, BUT HE DERIVES HIS BEING FROM THE FATHER.

ST. ATHANASIUS

THE WOMEN OF JERUSALEM

As Jesus carries his Cross through the crowded streets, a group of women weep for him. They are not apostles. They are not priests or rulers. They are the women of Jerusalem—ordinary bystanders, mothers and daughters. These are the witnesses moved by compassion.

And Jesus, battered and bruised, sees them. He turns to them—not in anger, not in indifference, but in love—and speaks words both tender and piercing: "Daughters of Jerusalem, do not weep for me, but weep for yourselves and for your children" (Lk 23:28).

This moment stands out in the Passion. It is the only recorded time, amid the violence and chaos of the Way of the Cross, that Jesus speaks to anyone outside his immediate circle. And he chooses these women—these unnamed, overlooked mourners.

Their tears are real. Their grief is honest. But Jesus, ever the prophet even in suffering, redirects their sorrow. He tells them to look deeper—not only at what is happening to him, but at what is happening to the world around them. "Weep for yourselves," he says—as a call to repentance, not rejection. As warning, not judgment. If this is what the world does to the innocent Lamb, what will happen when sin runs unchecked?

The women of Jerusalem represent all of us who look at the suffering Christ and feel sorrow—but stop short of conversion. It is not enough to feel pity. Christ wants our hearts. He desires not only our compassion but our repentance.

REFLECT

1. The women's compassion for Jesus was genuine, but he redirected it toward repentance. Do you sometimes mistake feelings about Christ for actual conversion to him? How can you move from emotion to transformation?
2. Jesus's warning implies that rejecting him has consequences for generations. How do your choices of faith or sin affect those who will follow you—children, godchildren, younger believers watching your example?
3. Pity alone could not save these women, but repentance could. Where is God asking you to stop merely "feeling sorry" for the brokenness of the world and start taking concrete steps toward holiness?

PRAY

LORD JESUS, YOU TURNED TO THE WOMEN OF JERUSALEM WITH LOVE AND TRUTH. YOU CALLED THEM BEYOND SORROW INTO REPENTANCE. TURN MY HEART AWAY FROM EMPTY SENTIMENT, AND TEACH ME TO SEE MY SIN AS YOU SEE IT. GIVE ME TEARS THAT LEAD TO CHANGE AND A LOVE FOR YOU THAT ENDURES. AMEN.

THIRD WEEK OF LENT

FRIDAY

HE IS HUNGRY AND EXHAUSTED, WEARY AND THIRSTY; HE FEARS AND FLEES AND IS TROUBLED WHEN HE PRAYS. HE SLEEPS ON A PILLOW, YET AS GOD HE HAS A NATURE THAT DOES NOT KNOW SLEEPING. HE ASKS TO BE EXCUSED THE SUFFERING OF THE CUP, YET HE WAS PRESENT IN THE WORLD FOR THIS VERY REASON. IN HIS AGONY, HE SWEATS AND AN ANGEL STRENGTHENS HIM, YET HE STRENGTHENS THOSE WHO BELIEVE IN HIM AND HAS TAUGHT THEM BY HIS EXAMPLE TO TREAT DEATH WITH CONTEMPT.

ST. HIPPOLYTUS OF ROME

THE ANGEL IN GETHSEMANE

In the Garden of Gethsemane, the weight of the coming Passion bears down on him—not just the pain of the Cross but also the sorrow of sin, the loneliness of abandonment, the silence of the Father. He prays, "Father, if you are willing, remove this cup from me; yet, not my will but yours be done" (Lk 22:42).

And in that moment, when even the disciples cannot stay awake with him, an angel appears.

Luke's gospel alone records this mysterious figure: "Then an angel from heaven appeared to him and gave him strength" (Lk 22:43).

It is not the first time angels have ministered to Jesus. At the start of his earthly life, they sang over the fields of Bethlehem to announce his birth. In the desert, after forty days of fasting and temptation, angels came and tended to him (Mt 4:11). And now, at the threshold of his Passion, one comes again—not to rescue him from suffering but to console him.

The angel in Gethsemane does not remove the cup. He does not silence the mob or turn back Judas. He does not lift Jesus out of the garden.

How often we ask for escape when what we truly need is strength.

God still sends his angels. Not always to change our circumstances—but to sustain us.

Perhaps you are in your own Gethsemane—a place of loneliness, confusion, or fear. Perhaps you are praying for the cup to pass. The angel who came to Jesus can fortify you.

In the end, the presence of the angel in the garden reminds us that Heaven never forgets the suffering of earth. God does not always spare us from pain, but he never leaves us alone in it.

REFLECT

1. Angels ministered to Jesus at key moments of his mission—at his birth, after his fasting, and before his Passion. What "angels" has God sent into your life—people, events, words—that gave you the courage to keep going?
2. The angel's appearance reminds us that Heaven sees and cares for earth's pain. How might remembering this truth change the way you face your own Gethsemane moments?

PRAY

LORD JESUS, IN THE GARDEN, YOU ACCEPTED THE FATHER'S WILL. YOU DID NOT REFUSE THE CROSS, BUT YOU RECEIVED STRENGTH FROM HEAVEN TO BEAR IT. SEND ME YOUR CONSOLATION IN MY TRIALS. HELP ME TO SEE THE ANGELS YOU PLACE ALONG MY PATH—MESSENGERS OF COURAGE, SIGNS OF YOUR LOVE. LET ME ALSO BE AN ANGEL TO OTHERS, BRINGING STRENGTH WHERE I CANNOT BRING ESCAPE. AMEN.

THIRD WEEK OF LENT

SATURDAY

WHEN HEROD WANTED TO SEE HIM WORK WONDERS, HE WAS SILENT AND PERFORMED NONE BECAUSE HEROD'S CRUELTY DID NOT MERIT TO BEHOLD THE DIVINE AND THE LORD SHUNNED BOASTING. PERHAPS HEROD PREFIGURES ALL THE IMPIOUS, WHO IF THEY DID NOT BELIEVE IN THE LAW AND THE PROPHETS CANNOT SEE THE MIRACULOUS WORKS OF CHRIST IN THE GOSPEL EITHER.

ST. AMBROSE

HEROD ANTIPAS

Herod is one of the most chilling—and most tragic—figures in the Passion. This is the Herod who beheaded John the Baptist. This is the Herod who heard the rumors about Jesus and wondered if John had come back from the dead. This is the Herod to whom Jesus sent a message: "Go and tell that fox . . ." (Lk 13:32).

It's not a compliment. In scripture and ancient culture, a fox isn't admired as clever—it is sly, opportunistic, and destructive. A fox raids the vineyard at night, taking what it can and vanishing. Herod is exactly that: a man who destroys what is good for the sake of his own appetites, always working in the shadows, always calculating how to keep his power.

When Jesus calls him "that fox," he is both naming Herod's cunning and unmasking his cowardice. A fox is not a lion; it doesn't fight openly—it slinks; it avoids risk. Herod had John the Baptist executed, but only after maneuvering himself into a situation where he could claim it wasn't really his decision. Even in the Passion, Herod will not take responsibility for judgment.

When Pilate hears that Jesus is a Galilean, he sees a way out. He sends him to Herod. Here, at last, is the moment Herod has been waiting for. Luke tells us Herod is "very glad" to see Jesus—glad, not because he wants the truth, but because "he had been wanting to see him for a long time . . . and was hoping to see him perform some sign" (Lk 23:8). Herod wants a show. He wants the fox's version of religion: something entertaining, impressive, but ultimately safe—something that never threatens the burrow where he hides his sins.

Jesus will have none of it. He answers Herod with silence, a judgment more eloquent than any accusation. In that silence, Jesus shows that he is not here to perform, to pander, to play Herod's games.

Herod's response is telling. Frustrated, he and his soldiers mock Jesus, dress him in a splendid robe, and send him back to Pilate. Like the fox, Herod takes what pleasure he can in damaging what is beautiful, then slips away before the decisive act.

Herod's tragedy is that he meets Jesus face-to-face and walks away unchanged. He hears no word, sees no sign, and so remains the same sly, self-protecting ruler he has always been. The lion of Judah stands before him, and all he sees is a prisoner to be mocked.

Jesus's path, however, is the opposite of the fox's. The fox clings to its den; the Son of Man has nowhere to lay his head. The fox takes what it can; the Lamb gives all he has. The fox lives by cunning; the Christ lives—and dies—by truth.

This Lent, may Jesus unmask the fox-like instincts in us.

REFLECT

1. Herod wanted to see Jesus perform a sign, but he had no intention of following him. Are you tempted to treat the Gospel as interesting rather than life-changing—something to discuss, read about, or admire, but not to obey?
2. Herod had silenced John the Baptist rather than repent. Are there areas of your life where you "keep Jesus at a distance" because you fear what he might ask you to change?
3. Herod grew bored and disappointed when Jesus did not answer. When God seems silent in prayer, do you grow restless, give up, or look for spiritual "quick fixes"? Or do you trust that his silence may be an invitation to deeper faith?

PRAY

LORD JESUS, YOU STOOD BEFORE HEROD IN SILENCE, REFUSING TO BE REDUCED TO A SPECTACLE. FORGIVE ME FOR THE TIMES I HAVE SOUGHT SIGNS INSTEAD OF SEEKING YOU. GIVE ME A HEART THAT LOVES THE TRUTH MORE THAN COMFORT, THAT LISTENS WHEN YOU SPEAK, AND THAT REPENTS WHEN YOU CONFRONT MY SIN. THIS LENT, STRIP AWAY MY PRIDE AND MY SELF-PROTECTION SO THAT I MAY WELCOME YOU AS MY KING. AMEN.

FOURTH WEEK OF LENT

The Children in Jerusalem

FOURTH WEEK OF LENT

SUNDAY

EVEN AS THE ROAD TO HELL IS LINED WITH ALL THE VICES, AND ESPECIALLY PRIDE, ALL THE VIRTUES LEAD TOWARD THE KINGDOM OF HEAVEN, AND ESPECIALLY HUMILITY. FOR THE ROOT OF ALL EVIL IS PRIDE, AND THE ROOT OF ALL GOOD IS HUMILITY. IT IS ONLY FITTING THAT ONE WHO EXALTS HIMSELF SHALL BE HUMBLED, AND ONE WHO HUMBLES HIMSELF SHALL BE EXALTED.

OPUS IMPERFECTUM IN MATTHAEUM

HUMILITY

Lent is the season when Jesus invites us to walk the downward road—the road that goes low before it rises. St. Paul says that Christ, "though he was in the form of God, did not regard equality with God as something to be exploited, but emptied himself, . . . humbled himself and became obedient to the point of death—even death on a cross" (Phil 2:6–8).

For Jesus, humility wasn't a trick for winning followers. It was the mission of the Incarnation.

But we struggle with this.

Real humility starts with God. It's remembering that *everything*—every breath, every talent, every grace—is a gift. St. Thomas Aquinas states point-blank, "The root of pride is found to consist in man not being, in some way, subject to God and his rule." Everything we have, we have received. This is the instinct that led St. Catherine of Siena to say to God, "I am she who is not, and you are he who is."

Importantly, humility doesn't mean denying the good in us. St. Francis de Sales warns against a "false and silly humility" that refuses to see the gifts God has placed in us. Those gifts, he says, should be recognized—so that we may glorify God who gave them. True humility leads to *generosity*: a trust in God that gives us courage to undertake whatever he commands, no matter how difficult. If humility makes us distrust ourselves, generosity makes us trust him.

The effect of humility is that it changes how we see others. Not only does pride distort our relationship with God, but, according to Aquinas, "sometimes it is also contrary to the love of our neighbor; when, namely, a man sets himself inordinately above his neighbor." There's always something in someone else worth reverencing, because God put it there. We are, in the Gospel, subject to one another.

Think of St. Thérèse of Lisieux and her "little way." She didn't chase great deeds. She chose hidden sacrifices, accepted misunderstandings without defense, and loved without demanding recognition. Her humility wasn't weakness—it was freedom.

In the end, humility, like poverty, is a prayer we hesitate to make because we're afraid of losing something. But in the Gospel, humility isn't loss—it's gain. It sets us free from the exhausting work of defending our ego. It unites us to others. It strengthens the will for self-gift. And most of all, it makes us resemble Jesus.

This Lent, what if we prayed for that? The courage to be small. The grace to be content with truth, not appearances. The joy of being overlooked, if it means we're walking in his footsteps. For on the far side of humility is the one exaltation that matters—when the Father lifts us up with Christ, and every knee bows, every tongue confesses that Jesus Christ is Lord.

REFLECT

1. Jesus didn't cling to his rights or status—he "emptied himself" and chose the low road. Where is he inviting you to take a step down? What would it look like to say yes?
2. St. Catherine of Siena said to God, "I am she who is not, and you are he who is." How does that truth change the way you see yourself, your gifts, and even your failures?
3. St. Francis de Sales says it's false humility to pretend we have no gifts. How can you use more intentionally your gifts for his glory instead of your own recognition?

PRAY

LORD JESUS, YOU WHO ARE GENTLE AND HUMBLE OF HEART, TEACH ME TO WALK YOUR LOWLY ROAD. HELP ME TO SEE EVERY BREATH, EVERY TALENT, EVERY GRACE AS A GIFT FROM YOU—AND TO SPEND THOSE GIFTS FREELY IN SERVICE, WITHOUT SEEKING MY OWN PRAISE. GIVE ME THE COURAGE TO BE OVERLOOKED, THE JOY TO SERVE IN SECRET, AND THE TRUST TO PLACE MY WHOLE WORTH IN YOUR LOVE ALONE. AMEN.

FOURTH WEEK OF LENT

MONDAY

WITH THAT HUMILITY THAT TAUGHT US ALSO TO BE HUMBLE, HE STILL CALLED HIM A PRIEST WHOM HE KNEW TO BE SACRILEGIOUS. ALSO UNDER THE VERY STING OF HIS PASSION, WHEN HE HAD RECEIVED A BLOW AND IT WAS SAID TO HIM, "DO YOU ANSWER THE HIGH PRIEST IN THIS WAY?" HE SAID NOTHING REPROACHFULLY AGAINST THE PERSON OF THE HIGH PRIEST. RATHER, HE MAINTAINED HIS OWN INNOCENCE. . . . ALL OF THE THINGS, THEREFORE, WERE DONE BY HIM HUMBLY AND PATIENTLY SO THAT WE MIGHT HAVE AN EXAMPLE OF HUMILITY AND PATIENCE.

ST. CYPRIAN

ANNAS, FORMER HIGH PRIEST

After his betrayal in Gethsemane, Jesus is taken to Annas, the former high priest and patriarch of the ruling priestly family. It is just the beginning of a long and sorrowful night. Though no longer officially in office, Annas still has a great deal of influence. The Gospel of John tells us that Jesus was taken to him first, as if to be inspected before being passed along like a criminal to Caiaphas, his son-in-law, and then on to the Romans (Jn 18:13). He is the power behind the throne, the patriarch of a priestly dynasty, with sons and sons-in-law in high places. The Sanhedrin moves in step with his will.

What a moment: The eternal High Priest, the Word-made-flesh, stands bound before a man clinging to borrowed authority. Annas is robed in earthly power, surrounded by guards and servants. Jesus, bound like a criminal, stands in silence before him, offering no defense.

Jesus Christ is not merely a holier priest.

His priesthood does not rest on lineage, ritual, or temple service. It flows from the mystery of who he is: the divine Word made flesh. His humanity is sanctified not by any external grace but by the uncreated grace of the hypostatic union—the perfect and eternal union of the human and divine natures in his one divine person. This union constitutes the very nature of his priesthood.

Annas cannot comprehend such a priesthood. He wields inherited authority but stands powerless before the one who is the source of all priestly power. For while every other priest offers what is holy, Christ alone is the Holy One who offers himself.

Bound before Annas, he reveals the radiant beauty of a priesthood rooted not in prestige but in perfect union with the Father. The priesthood of Jesus Christ is not a priesthood of self-preservation but of self-gift.

REFLECT

1. Annas clung to influence and power even after his official role had ended. When have you been tempted to hold on to positions, titles, or roles because they gave you a sense of control or importance, not letting them go in humility?
2. Jesus stood bound before Annas, yet his authority came from his perfect union with the Father. How does this challenge the ways you define authority and success in your own life?

PRAY

LORD JESUS, TRUE AND ETERNAL HIGH PRIEST, YOU STOOD BOUND BEFORE ANNAS, DEFENDING NOTHING OF YOURSELF BUT THE TRUTH. STRIP AWAY MY FALSE SECURITIES, MY PRIDE, AND MY HUNGER FOR HUMAN APPROVAL. TEACH ME THE HUMILITY THAT STANDS FIRM BEFORE WORLDLY POWER AND THE PATIENCE THAT ENDURES MISUNDERSTANDING. AMEN.

FOURTH WEEK OF LENT

TUESDAY

THERE ARE THOSE WHO STILL HAVE THORNS WITH WHICH THEY CROWN AND DISHONOR JESUS, THOSE, NAMELY, WHO ARE CHOKED BY THE CARES AND RICHES AND PLEASURES OF LIFE AND, THOUGH THEY HAVE RECEIVED THE WORD OF GOD, DO NOT BRING IT TO PERFECTION. WE MUST BEWARE, THEREFORE, LEST WE ALSO, AS CROWNING JESUS WITH THORNS OF OUR OWN, SHOULD BE ENTERED IN THE GOSPEL . . . AND READ HOW HE IS DISHONORED AND MOCKED AND BEATEN BY US.

ORIGEN

THE MOCKING SOLDIERS

The soldiers who mocked Christ had seen many criminals before. They had guarded prisoners, whipped and cursed and struck those who had been condemned. They were no strangers to executions and crucifixions. But something about Jesus invited more than their typical disdain.

They twisted together a crown of thorns and pressed it into his head. They draped a faded purple cloak over his torn shoulders—a robe not of majesty but of ridicule. They placed a reed in his hand, pretending it was a scepter. And then they knelt before him, laughing.

"Hail, King of the Jews!" the soldiers cried (Mk 15:16–19).

What bitter irony. Every object the soldiers used to mock Jesus was, in fact, a sign of truth. The crown, though made of thorns, pointed to his kingship, a reign not of conquest but of suffering love. The cloak, a discarded soldier's garment, hinted at the royal robes of the Messiah, though here it was soaked in blood rather than glory. And the reed, fragile and breakable, served as a scepter, yet even that symbol spoke to the kind of authority Christ came to wield: not by force but by mercy.

They did not realize that their parody of kingship was, in fact, a revelation.

Jesus was silent in the face of their scorn. He allowed their mockery. He received it. And in doing so, he exposed the cruelty of a world that does not know how to respond to holiness except with violence or laughter.

And he loved them still.

That's the mystery: He endured their ridicule not because he was weak but because he was strong enough to bear it. The very soldiers who mocked him were the ones he came to save. The very men who spat upon him were the ones he carried in his heart to the Cross. The very hands that wove the crown were the hands he stretched out his arms to save.

REFLECT

1. The thorns pressed into the head of Our Lord came from a world that he created good yet was marred by sin. What "thorns" in your life—habits, attachments, sins—still pierce Christ's heart and need to be surrendered to him?
2. Jesus endured humiliation without defending himself, revealing a strength rooted in love. How do you usually respond when your dignity is challenged or your reputation attacked, and what would it take to answer as Christ did?
3. Jesus loved even the men who mocked him. How can you learn to love those who have hurt, ridiculed, or opposed you, and to pray sincerely for their good?

PRAY

KING OF MERCY, CROWNED WITH THORNS FOR MY SAKE, FORGIVE ME FOR THE TIMES I HAVE DISHONORED YOU IN THOUGHT, WORD, OR ACTION. LET MY HANDS NO LONGER WOUND YOU BUT INSTEAD WEAVE A CROWN OF PRAISE BY MY FAITH, MY OBEDIENCE, AND MY LOVE. MAY I SEE IN EVERY TRIAL A SHARE IN YOUR ROYAL DIGNITY, AND MAY MY LIFE PROCLAIM, "HAIL, CHRIST THE KING," UNTIL I BEHOLD YOU CROWNED IN GLORY. AMEN.

FOURTH WEEK OF LENT

WEDNESDAY

HOW CAN THEY BE FALSE WITNESSES IF THEY SAID WHAT WE READ THE LORD HAD SAID BEFORE? BECAUSE A FALSE WITNESS TAKES THE TRUTH AND TWISTS ITS MEANING. THE LORD HAD SPOKEN OF THE TEMPLE OF HIS BODY, BUT THEY FALSELY ACCUSED HIM WITH THOSE VERY WORDS.

ST. JEROME

FALSE WITNESSES BEFORE THE SANHEDRIN

In the final hours of Jesus's life, testimony plays a crucial role—but not the kind that brings justice. As Jesus is brought before the chief priests, the gospels tell us that many came forward with false testimony against him, hoping to secure his death: "We heard him say, 'I will destroy this temple that is made with hands, and in three days I will build another, not made with hands'" (Mk 14:58). Their words twist the truth. Their accusations are rehearsed lies. Even so, their stories don't add up. Lies rarely do.

Compare their testimony to that of John the Baptist. When religious leaders question him—"Who are you?"—John answers with clarity and humility. "I am not the Messiah," he says. "I am the voice of one crying out in the wilderness, 'Make straight the way of the Lord'" (Jn 1:19–20, 23). His whole mission is to prepare the way for another. John points beyond himself to Christ, the Lamb of God who takes away the sin of the world. John came to bear witness to the light. And so must we.

But the greatest testimony in the gospels comes from Jesus himself. "Very truly, I tell you," he says, "we speak of what we know and testify to what we have seen" (Jn 3:11). Christ testifies to the Father. He reveals what he has seen from eternity. He speaks what he has always known.

"Even if I testify on my own behalf," Jesus says, "my testimony is valid because I know where I have come from and where I am going" (Jn 8:14). His words and works do not need the approval of human judges. His mission is not upheld by human courts. The Father himself testifies on his behalf, through the miracles, the signs, and ultimately through the Cross.

The Cross is the final word of Christ's testimony—proof that the love of the Father endures even through death. And at the foot of the Cross, the beloved disciple will testify to what he has seen: "His testimony is true, and he knows that he tells the truth" so that like him, we believe (Jn 19:35).

God is Truth. There is no darkness in him. And yet, how easily we let our thoughts be shaped by false voices. If our witness to Christ is not clear and visible, we are not so different from the false witnesses who stood before him on the morning of his trial.

REFLECT

1. The false witnesses spoke with confidence, yet their words were empty of truth. When have you been careless with your words, allowing exaggeration, gossip, or half-truths to pass your lips?
2. The lies told about the Lord were designed to bring harm. Have you ever allowed fear, resentment, or self-interest to distort your witness to Christ, whether by what you said or by your silence?

PRAY

LORD JESUS, FAITHFUL WITNESS OF THE FATHER, YOU STOOD BEFORE FALSE ACCUSERS WITHOUT DECEIT. PURIFY MY WORDS AND GUARD MY LIPS FROM SPEAKING ANYTHING UNTRUE. GIVE ME THE COURAGE TO TESTIFY TO YOU IN SEASON AND OUT OF SEASON, EVEN WHEN THE TRUTH IS COSTLY. LET MY LIFE BEAR WITNESS TO THE CROSS SO THAT OTHERS MAY BELIEVE IN YOU AND LIVE. AMEN.

FOURTH WEEK OF LENT

THURSDAY

THE LORD TEACHES THAT WE CANNOT ENTER THE KINGDOM OF HEAVEN UNLESS WE REVERT TO THE NATURE OF CHILDREN. . . . HE HAS CALLED CHILDREN ALL WHO BELIEVE THROUGH THE FAITH OF LISTENING. FOR CHILDREN FOLLOW THEIR FATHER, LOVE THEIR MOTHER, DO NOT KNOW HOW TO WISH ILL ON THEIR NEIGHBOR, SHOW NO CONCERN FOR WEALTH, ARE NOT PROUD, DO NOT HATE, DO NOT LIE, BELIEVE WHAT HAS BEEN SAID AND HOLD WHAT THEY HEAR AS TRUTH.

ST. HILARY OF POITIERS

THE CHILDREN CARRYING PALM BRANCHES

As Jesus rode into Jerusalem on a humble colt, the streets filled with shouts of joy. Cloaks were thrown on the road, branches torn from trees, and at the center of it all—the children. They were the first to run. Their little feet pattered over the stones, voices rising in song. "Hosanna to the Son of David!" they cried, their words loud, bright, unfiltered (Mt 21:15). It was not a carefully rehearsed chant; it was the spontaneous joy of children who had heard that the King was coming and believed it was true.

Imagine them in procession—like children on a playground, full of energy and delight. They dart between adults, waving palm branches like banners, dancing in circles, flinging cloaks about them, skipping, laughing, singing, calling out to one another. Their praise is not forced or self-conscious. It flows from the heart. They don't need to understand every prophecy or theological detail. They see Jesus, and they rejoice.

The Pharisees, uncomfortable with such unbridled praise, demand silence. But Jesus does not hush them. He honors them. He recognizes the beauty of their worship. He receives it as pure.

These are the ones of whom he had earlier said, "Let the little children come to me, and do not stop them; for it is to such as these that the kingdom of heaven belongs" (Mt 19:14). Now, they come—not in quiet piety but in movement, laughter, and song. They are the prophets of Palm Sunday, the first heralds of the King.

Remember that Jesus taught his disciples, "Truly I tell you, unless you change and become like children, you will never enter the kingdom of heaven. Whoever becomes humble like this child is the greatest in the kingdom of heaven" (Mt 18:3–4). On Palm Sunday, we see that teaching come to life in the children in procession. In them, we glimpse the kind of soul that welcomes the King: a soul uncluttered by pride, free to rejoice, free to believe.

This Lent, their joy invites us to return to a simpler faith. Not a childish one, but a childlike one. With faith not tangled in fear or cynicism. With hearts ready to run, to dance, to praise.

REFLECT

1. The children ran to Jesus without hesitation or self-consciousness. When have you felt the freedom to praise God without worrying about what others might think?
2. The Pharisees wanted to silence their joy. What voices—whether from within or from others—try to quiet your praise or dampen your hope, and how can you resist them?
3. Childlike faith is marked by trust, humility, and joy. Which of these qualities is strongest in you right now, and which needs to grow? What concrete steps can you take this Lent to return to simplicity of heart and clarity of faith?

PRAY

*LORD JESUS, SON OF DAVID,
RECEIVE MY HOSANNA AS YOU ONCE
RECEIVED THE JOYFUL SHOUTS
OF THE CHILDREN OF JERUSALEM.
SWEEP AWAY THE CLUTTER OF PRIDE
AND FEAR FROM MY HEART SO THAT
I MAY WELCOME YOU WITH JOY.
MAY MY PRAISE BE PURE AND MY
FAITH BE SIMPLE, UNTIL I ENTER
THE KINGDOM YOU HAVE PREPARED.
AMEN.*

FOURTH WEEK OF LENT

FRIDAY

AS THEY WERE "LOOKING ON," SO WE TOO GAZE ON HIS WOUNDS AS HE HANGS. WE SEE HIS BLOOD AS HE DIES. WE SEE THE PRICE OFFERED BY THE REDEEMER, TOUCH THE SCARS OF HIS RESURRECTION. HE BOWS HIS HEAD, AS IF TO KISS YOU. HIS HEART IS MADE BARE OPEN, AS IT WERE, IN LOVE TO YOU. HIS ARMS ARE EXTENDED THAT HE MAY EMBRACE YOU. HIS WHOLE BODY IS DISPLAYED FOR YOUR REDEMPTION.

ST. AUGUSTINE

SALOME, MOTHER OF JAMES AND JOHN

Salome once knelt before Jesus with a bold request—a mother's plea for greatness. She asked that her sons, James and John, might sit at his right and his left in his kingdom (Mt 20:20–21). It was an audacious request, perhaps made in love but colored by human ambition. Like so many who followed Jesus, Salome misunderstood his kingdom. She longed for thrones; he spoke of a Cross. She sought honor; he offered a cup of suffering.

Jesus did not rebuke her harshly. He simply said, "You do not know what you are asking" (Mt 20:22). And indeed, she did not. But at the foot of the Cross, her understanding began to change.

There, beneath the darkened sky, Salome saw with painful clarity what true glory looked like. It was not what she had imagined. There was no royal court, no golden throne, no crown of jewels. Instead, there was a battered man—bloodied, gasping, nailed to the wooden beams. And beside him, not princes in splendor but two criminals. This was the place of his enthronement: a hill outside the city, marked by rejection and death.

As she stood there, watching Jesus die, how heavy her earlier words must have felt. How bitter the memory of that request: "Declare that these two sons of mine will sit, one at your right hand and one at your left, in your kingdom" (Mt 20:21). She had asked for proximity to greatness. Now she saw that greatness in the suffering Christ, and it must have broken her heart.

Her ambition was not evil; it sprang from love. But at the Cross, it was purified. At last, she began to see—to be close to Jesus is to suffer with him. To share in his kingdom is to share in his sacrifice. To follow him is not to rise above others but to go lower—into the places of pain, rejection, and loss—and to find him there.

If she was ashamed of her request, she did not let it keep her from him. With Mary Magdalene and Mary the mother of James, she carried spices to anoint the broken body of her Lord. And in so doing, she became one of the first witnesses of the resurrection (Mt 28:1).

At the foot of the Cross, Salome learned that her deepest desire—to be near Christ—would be answered. But it would be answered in God's way, not hers. And that makes all the difference.

REFLECT

1. Salome's request for her sons came from love but was clouded by ambition. How have your prayers sometimes been shaped more by what you want than by what God desires for you?
2. Salome did not let her earlier misunderstanding keep her away. How can you let go of past mistakes and still draw close to Christ with confidence?

PRAY

LORD JESUS, YOU GENTLY CORRECTED SALOME'S AMBITION AND INVITED HER TO DRINK FROM YOUR CHALICE. PURIFY MY DESIRES SO THAT I MAY SEEK ONLY TO BE WITH YOU, WHETHER IN JOY OR IN TRIAL. TEACH ME TO SEE TRUE GREATNESS IN HUMILITY, TRUE HONOR IN SERVICE, AND TRUE GLORY IN THE CROSS. LET MY HEART REST IN YOUR WILL ALONE. AMEN.

FOURTH WEEK OF LENT

SATURDAY

THERE ARE MANY EVEN NOW FIGHTING AGAINST JESUS WITH SPIRITUAL SWORDS AND STAVES OF EVIL. . . . JESUS ALWAYS GETS THE BETTER OF THEIR PLOTS, ALTHOUGH FOR A TIME HE RECEIVES THEIR ATTACKS ON HIM IN ORDER THAT THE SINS OF THOSE WHO PLOT AGAINST HIM MAY BE COMPLETE AND THE WICKEDNESS OF THEIR WILL AGAINST THE TRUTH OF GOD'S ONLY-BEGOTTEN, THE WORD, MAY BE MADE KNOWN.

ORIGEN

THE TEMPLE GUARDS

They came with swords and clubs, lanterns and torches. Into the quiet darkness of Gethsemane, the temple guards marched with cautious steps, fearful of tripping on roots or stumbling into unseen hollows. Every step was careful, every eye searching the shadows. They feared the dark. But they did not fear the deeper darkness they carried within.

The light of the world stood before them, calm and unarmed. And they were blind.

Christ is not merely a bearer of light. He *is* the light, the radiance of God breaking into a world clouded by sin. From the opening of John's gospel, we are told, "The light shines in the darkness, and the darkness did not overcome it" (Jn 1:5).

This is no metaphor. Christ illuminates the deepest recesses of the human heart. He reveals what is true, what is good, what is eternal. Without him, we cannot even know the depths of our own hearts. And on that night in Gethsemane, the guards—men charged with protecting the sacred—rejected the light and bound him in chains.

In a deeper irony, these were not just any soldiers; they were temple guards, sent by the chief priests. "Judas brought a detachment of soldiers together with police from the chief priests and the Pharisees, and they came there with lanterns and torches and weapons" (Jn 18:3). They served the holy place in Jerusalem, where sacrifices were offered and God's presence dwelt. And yet they failed to see that they were standing before the true Temple: the living, breathing dwelling place of God.

Jesus had said, "Destroy this temple, and in three days I will raise it up," speaking of his body (Jn 2:19–21). The true meeting place of heaven and earth was not behind the veil in the sanctuary; it was there in the garden.

The Light they claimed to search for was the Light they extinguished. The Temple they defended was only a shadow of the one they condemned.

REFLECT

1. The guards served the Temple but failed to recognize the true Temple standing before them. What good and holy things in your life risk becoming substitutes for Christ himself?
2. These guards acted under orders, yet each was responsible for his choice. How do you discern between obedience to human authority and fidelity to God's will?

PRAY

LIGHT OF THE WORLD, YOU STOOD UNARMED BEFORE THOSE WHO CAME TO BIND YOU, AND WITH A WORD YOU REVEALED YOUR DIVINITY. SHINE INTO MY DARKNESS AND SCATTER MY FEAR. LET ME NEVER RESIST YOUR PRESENCE BUT INSTEAD WELCOME YOU AS THE TRUE TEMPLE AND THE DWELLING PLACE OF GOD. AMEN.

FIFTH WEEK OF LENT

Matthew, the Tax Collector

FIFTH WEEK OF LENT

SUNDAY

THE DISCIPLES HAD NOT YET BEEN CLOTHED WITH THE POWER FROM ON HIGH, NEITHER HAD THEY RECEIVED THE STRENGTH THAT WAS TO INVIGORATE THEM AND IMPART COURAGE TO THEIR CHARACTER—I MEAN THE GIFT OF THE HOLY SPIRIT. THUS, THEY WERE NOT ABLE TO WRESTLE WITH DEATH AND ENGAGE IN A CONFLICT WITH TERRORS SO HARD TO FACE.

ST. CYRIL OF ALEXANDRIA

COURAGE

What does it mean to be courageous?

In the fifteenth century, the Dominican friar Bl. Anthony Neyrot was captured by pirates and taken to Tunis. There, under the strain of imprisonment and lured by the promise of comfort, he denied Christ, abandoned his vocation, and embraced Islam.

But God's mercy found him. Shaken by news of the death of his mentor and moved by a dream of the saint calling him back, Anthony repented, publicly sought forgiveness, and returned to the habit. Four days later, on Holy Thursday, he boldly professed his faith before the ruler of Tunis and was executed.

We might think of courage as the stuff of epic movies, but the courage Christ calls us to often looks less like fanfare and more like faithfulness. It's the grace to keep saying yes to God when fear, pressure, or even common sense says no.

Lent puts courage front and center. Jesus sets his face toward Jerusalem, knowing the Cross awaits him. And his courage—love that will not turn back, even when the road runs through suffering—is still alive today in ordinary Catholics who are living extraordinary courage.

Think of Christians in the Middle East. Churches have been destroyed, communities scattered, yet the faithful remain. They know the cost of following Christ—and they've decided he's worth it.

Or think of pro-life witnesses who stand outside abortion clinics. The weather is harsh, and the words hurled at them are harsher. Yet they're there—praying, offering help, and quietly holding out hope.

Then there's the courage of faithful family life. It's not easy to teach Christ's vision of love and truth when classmates and media say otherwise. But parents who persevere are planting seeds of faith watered by their example and sacrifice.

And we can't forget the courage of speaking truth in the workplace. It might mean refusing to participate in something you know is wrong. It might even mean explaining your faith when you know it could cost you advancement or respect. This courage doesn't make headlines, but it's the kind Heaven notices.

Courage isn't just a personal trait—it's a virtue, one bolstered by grace. St. Thomas Aquinas calls it fortitude: the strength to endure and to persevere in the good, especially when it's hard or dangerous. Lent is a perfect time to ask the Lord to grow this virtue in us. Of all the virtues we need to cultivate today, courage is the most important.

Because courage isn't optional for a disciple. Whether we face open persecution, cultural pressure, or quiet temptation, the call is the same: Follow Christ, even when it costs something.

And here's the good news—he doesn't ask us to do it alone. The same Jesus who walked the road to Calvary and forgave from the Cross walks with us. And he gives us companions to remind us that we're part of a much bigger story.

REFLECT

1. When you see others falter or fail in their faith, do you respond with judgment or with the mercy that can help them return to Christ? How can you be an instrument of encouragement and reconciliation?
2. What concrete steps can you take this Lent to grow in the kind of courage that remains faithful under trial—through prayer, sacramental grace, and daily acts of self-denial?

PRAY

LORD JESUS, YOU FACED THE CROSS WITH STEADFAST LOVE, UNSHAKEN BY FEAR OR THE THREATS OF MEN. GRANT ME THE VIRTUE OF COURAGE, THE QUIET STRENGTH THAT REMAINS FAITHFUL IN TRIAL. MAKE ME WILLING TO LOSE WHAT THE WORLD PRIZES SO THAT I MAY GAIN WHAT YOU PROMISE. AMEN.

FIFTH WEEK OF LENT

MONDAY

THE LORD SAID THEY KNEW THE PLACE TO WHICH AND THE WAY WHEREBY HE WAS GOING. THOMAS DECLARES HE DOES NOT KNOW EITHER THE PLACE OR THE WAY. BUT THOMAS DOES NOT KNOW HE IS SPEAKING FALSELY. THEY KNEW, BUT THEY DID NOT KNOW THAT THEY KNEW. JESUS, HOWEVER, WILL CONVINCE THEM OF WHAT THEY ALREADY KNOW EVEN THOUGH THEY THEMSELVES IMAGINE THAT THEY ARE IGNORANT ABOUT IT.

ST. AUGUSTINE

THOMAS, CALLED "DIDYMUS"

When Jesus announced his return to Judea to raise Lazarus, the apostles hesitated. They knew the danger. The last time Jesus was there, the leaders had tried to stone him. But Thomas, often remembered only for his doubt, was the one who spoke with somber courage: "Let us also go, that we may die with him" (Jn 11:16).

It was a grim resolve. Thomas expected death. It was a willingness to follow Jesus into the shadows, not a triumphant declaration. If Jesus was going to die, then so would they. There is no Easter in his voice, no Resurrection hope, only loyalty in the face of looming loss.

Then, during the Last Supper, Jesus speaks words of comfort: "Do not let your hearts be troubled. . . . In my Father's house there are many dwelling places. . . . You know the way to the place where I am going." And Thomas, still honest, still unsure, replies, "Lord, we do not know where you are going. How can we know the way?" His words are not defiant but searching. And to him, Jesus gives one of the most beautiful revelations in all of scripture: "I am the way, and the truth, and the life" (Jn 14: 1–6).

Even so, after the Cross, Thomas disappears into silence like the rest of the disciples. And when the others proclaim the risen Christ, he resists: *Unless I see . . . unless I touch . . .* But Jesus, full of mercy, comes to him. He meets him not with scolding but with wounds. He invites Thomas to see, to touch, to believe. And here's the mystery: From Thomas—who once feared death, who once could not see the way—comes the most moving confession in the gospels: "My Lord and my God!" (Jn 20:25–28).

REFLECT

1. Thomas's statement "Let us also go, that we may die with him" comes from a place of loyalty, but one without Resurrection hope. In your own discipleship, when have you followed Christ more out of obligation or grim endurance than out of joyful expectation of his victory?
2. At the Last Supper, Thomas admits his confusion: "Lord, we do not know where you are going." How willing are you to bring your uncertainties, misunderstandings, or lack of clarity before God rather than pretending you have all the answers?

PRAY

LORD JESUS, YOU MET THOMAS IN HIS DOUBT AND TRANSFORMED HIS FEAR INTO BOLD CONFESSION. MEET ME IN MY UNCERTAINTY, MY HESITATIONS, AND MY SHADOWED PLACES. TAKE MY LOYALTY AND FILL IT WITH HOPE. GIVE ME EYES TO SEE YOU AS YOU ARE AND COURAGE TO FOLLOW WHEREVER YOU LEAD. MAY MY LIPS, LIKE THOMAS'S, PROCLAIM YOU AS MY LORD AND MY GOD. AMEN.

FIFTH WEEK OF LENT

TUESDAY

WHY ARE THESE THREE APOSTLES ALWAYS CHOSEN AND THE OTHERS SENT AWAY? . . . IT IS WRITTEN: "A THREE-PLY CORD IS NOT EASILY BROKEN." PETER IS CHOSEN AS ONE UPON WHOM THE CHURCH WOULD BE BUILT. JAMES IS THE FIRST OF THE APOSTLES TO BE CROWNED WITH MARTYRDOM. JOHN IS THE BELOVED DISCIPLE WHOSE LOVE PREFIGURES THE STATE OF VIRGINITY.

ST. JEROME

JAMES, SON OF ZEBEDEE

James, the son of Zebedee, knew closeness to Christ in a way few others did. He was among the first called—one moment mending nets with his brother John on the shore of Galilee, the next, leaving everything behind at Jesus's invitation (Mt 4:21–22).

With Peter and John, James belonged to Jesus's inner circle. He was there when Jesus raised Jairus's daughter (Mk 5:37). He climbed the mountain and saw the Lord transfigured in radiant light, flanked by Moses and Elijah, the voice of the Father thundering from the cloud: "This is my Son, the Beloved; listen to him" (Mk 9:7). And later, he was in Gethsemane on the night of Jesus's arrest. Jesus brought him deeper into the garden, saying to him, "I am deeply grieved, even to death; remain here, and stay awake with me" (Mt 26:38).

James witnessed Christ's glory and his trembling. He saw glimpses of both his divine majesty and his human anguish. Yet even so, when Jesus spoke of suffering, the chalice of his Passion, James did not yet understand. He and John asked for places of honor in the kingdom, still imagining power without pain. Still seeking greatness on their own terms.

But Jesus, with patient love, did not dismiss their request. Instead, he redirected it: "Are you able to drink the cup that I am about to drink?" (Mt 20:22). It is a question not of worthiness but of willingness. Jesus offers James the path not just of glory but of sacrifice—the path that Jesus himself would walk first.

In time, James would follow. He would learn that the path to the throne of glory is paved with thorns. He would learn that the chalice he once feared was, in truth, the cup of communion with Christ. And he would become the first apostle to die for the name of Jesus (Acts 12:2), a witness not only in word but in his blood: "For just as the sufferings of Christ are abundant for us, so also our consolation is abundant through Christ" (2 Cor 1:5).

REFLECT

1. James stood among the few who witnessed both Christ's transfiguration and his agony in Gethsemane. How do you respond when God gives you moments of glory and closeness—do you let them prepare you for future trials, or do you expect them to be the norm? How well are you allowing the mountaintop experiences in your faith to strengthen you for the valleys?
2. James was the first of the apostles to be martyred, yet he did not start his journey ready for such a cost. How might God be preparing you now for future trials or opportunities to witness for him in costly ways, and are you cooperating with that preparation?

PRAY

LORD JESUS, YOU CALLED JAMES FROM THE SEA TO THE MOUNTAIN, FROM THE MOUNTAIN TO THE GARDEN, AND FROM THE GARDEN TO THE CHALICE OF YOUR PASSION. TEACH ME TO FOLLOW YOU IN EVERY PLACE YOU LEAD. WHEN I AM TEMPTED TO SEEK ONLY GLORY, REMIND ME THAT THE PATH TO THE CROWN RUNS THROUGH THE CROSS. GIVE ME COURAGE TO DRINK THE CUP YOU PLACE IN MY HANDS, KNOWING IT IS THE CUP OF LOVE. AMEN.

FIFTH WEEK OF LENT

WEDNESDAY

NOT EVERYONE CAN BURY CHRIST. ALTHOUGH THE PIOUS WOMEN STAND FAR AWAY, BECAUSE THEY ARE PIOUS, THEY WATCH THE PLACE CLOSELY TO BRING OINTMENTS AND ANOINT HIM. [THEY] ARE THE LAST TO LEAVE THE TOMB AND THE FIRST TO RETURN TO IT.

ST. AMBROSE

JOANNA, WIFE OF CHUZA

Joanna knew the corridors of power. As the wife of Chuza, household manager to Herod Antipas, she had walked through palaces, stood in echoing marble halls, and heard the whispers of judgment from behind closed doors. She knew how the corridors of power worked—how men like Herod held court, how political threats were handled, and how calculating politicians crushed what they feared.

And still, she chose to follow Jesus.

He had healed her. We don't know how, only that his touch changed everything. From that moment, she stepped away from a life of comfort and status and joined the band of women who followed the Lord, providing for him out of their own means (Lk 8:1–3). Joanna became a disciple, one who walked the long roads with Christ, quietly offering to him all that she had.

She followed him not only in Galilee but to Jerusalem—into the heart of danger, into the hour of darkness.

We can only imagine what Joanna must have felt during those final days of Christ's life. She knew how Herod operated. Had she heard the rumors before the arrest? Had someone in the palace whispered to her that Jesus had become too dangerous? That Rome was watching? That the Galilean preacher's fate was already sealed?

Perhaps she hoped it could be stopped. Perhaps she wept when Herod, that petty tyrant, mocked the Lord and sent him back to Pilate dressed in a robe of scorn (Lk 23:11). Joanna had served this man's household. Now she saw him humiliate her Lord.

When the apostles hid, she watched where they laid the body. And early on the first day of the week, before dawn, Joanna came to the tomb with spices in hand and sorrow in her heart, prepared to anoint the body of the one who had given her back her life.

REFLECT

1. Joanna left a position of privilege in Herod's household to follow a Galilean preacher who was increasingly despised by the powerful. In your own life, where are you tempted to protect your reputation, status, or comfort instead of risking them for Christ?
2. Luke tells us that Joanna was among the women who supported Jesus's ministry out of their own means. What resources—time, money, influence, or talents—has Christ entrusted to you, and how are you currently using them to serve his mission?
3. Joanna saw firsthand the corrupt political forces that condemned Jesus. When you witness injustice or cruelty in your own circles, do you speak out, act quietly behind the scenes, or retreat into silence? What does true discipleship require of you in those moments?

PRAY

LORD JESUS, YOU HEALED JOANNA AND CALLED HER FROM THE HALLS OF EARTHLY POWER TO THE ROAD OF HUMBLE DISCIPLESHIP. GIVE ME HER COURAGE TO FOLLOW YOU WHEN IT COSTS ME COMFORT, REPUTATION, OR SECURITY. AND WHEN THE NIGHT IS LONG AND HOPE SEEMS BURIED, LET ME RISE EARLY—LIKE JOANNA—TO MEET YOU IN THE DAWN OF YOUR RESURRECTION. AMEN.

FIFTH WEEK OF LENT

THURSDAY

PHILIP DID NOT DENY THAT THE FATHER COULD BE SEEN BUT ONLY ASKED THAT HE MIGHT SEE HIM. HE DID NOT ASK THAT THE FATHER SHOULD BE UNVEILED SO THAT HE COULD SEE HIM WITH HIS BODILY EYES, BUT THAT HE MIGHT HAVE SOME FURTHER INDICATION . . . CONCERNING HOW THE FATHER COULD BE SEEN. FOR HE HAD SEEN THE SON UNDER THE ASPECT OF HUMANITY BUT CANNOT UNDERSTAND HOW HE COULD THEREBY HAVE SEEN THE FATHER.

ST. HILARY OF POITIERS

PHILIP OF BETHSAIDA

"Lord, show us the Father, and we will be satisfied" (Jn 14:8). Philip's longing is honest. His words at the Last Supper rise from a heart that has followed Jesus, listened closely, stayed near—and still hungers for more. "Show us the Father," he says, "and we will be satisfied."

This is not the first time Philip has struggled to see beyond the surface. Earlier in John's gospel, at the feeding of the five thousand, Jesus had turned to him with a question: "Where are we to buy bread for these people to eat?" (Jn 6:5). It was a test, an invitation to trust. But Philip does the math. His answer is practical, even defeated: "Six months' wages would not buy enough bread for each of them to get a little" (Jn 6:7). His imagination remains bound by the world's logic: by scarcity, by calculation, by what is humanly possible.

And now, at the Last Supper, that same struggle appears again. Philip wants clarity. He wants to see the Father with his own eyes. And Jesus, with patient love, responds, "Whoever has seen me has seen the Father" (Jn 14:9). The God Philip longs to see is already before him: breaking bread, washing feet, preparing to suffer. The true miracle isn't just that Jesus fed a crowd; it's that, in him, the fullness of God has come near in flesh and blood.

Lent confronts this same tension in us. We want to believe, but we often live by the logic of the world: We worry about what's "enough"; we measure everything by what we can see and count. We miss Christ's presence already with us, calling us to deeper faith. We have not been abandoned. The Father is near.

Philip reminds us that even close followers can miss the glory before them. And yet, Jesus continues to draw them—and us—deeper. Not into simple formulas or trite answers, but into a relationship with the living God. In his Passion, the suffering

Savior reveals the Father's heart in every wound and every act of love.

REFLECT

1. Philip wanted clarity and certainty before he could rest content in his faith: "Show us the Father, and we will be satisfied." In your own journey, what assurances or signs do you still think you need from God before you can fully trust him?
2. Jesus tells Philip, "Whoever has seen me has seen the Father." How might you be missing God's presence in your life because you expect him to appear in ways that fit your own expectations rather than in the humble, ordinary, or even challenging realities before you?
3. At the feeding of the five thousand, Philip calculated what was possible in human terms rather than trusting in divine abundance. In what areas of your life do you still rely on your own limited calculations instead of stepping out in faith that God will provide?

PRAY

LORD JESUS, YOU ARE THE WAY TO THE FATHER, YET I OFTEN SEARCH AS IF HE WERE FAR AWAY. OPEN MY EYES TO SEE THE FATHER IN YOU—IN YOUR MERCY, YOUR SACRIFICE, AND YOUR LOVE POURED OUT. FREE ME FROM THE TYRANNY OF MY OWN CALCULATIONS, AND TEACH ME TO TRUST IN YOUR ABUNDANCE. SHOW ME THE FATHER, LORD, AND I WILL BE SATISFIED. AMEN.

FIFTH WEEK OF LENT

FRIDAY

WHEN JESUS IS ATTACKED FOR MIXING WITH SINNERS, AND TAKING AS HIS DISCIPLE A DESPISED TAX COLLECTOR, ONE MIGHT ASK: WHAT COULD HE POSSIBLY GAIN BY DOING SO? ONLY THE SALVATION OF SINNERS. TO BLAME JESUS FOR MINGLING WITH SINNERS WOULD BE LIKE BLAMING A PHYSICIAN FOR STOOPING DOWN OVER SUFFERING AND PUTTING UP WITH VILE SMELLS IN ORDER TO HEAL THE SICK.

ST. GREGORY OF NAZIANZUS

MATTHEW, THE TAX COLLECTOR

Matthew once lived for gain: counting coins, guarding ledgers, calculating the cost of every decision. As a tax collector, he was a man of plain figures, not mysteries. Then one day, Christ passed by and simply said, "Follow me" (Mk 2:14). And Matthew got up. No questions. No conditions. He left the table, his numbers, and the life that had always made sense in order to follow a Teacher who lived by a new logic.

It is this same Matthew who gives us the Sermon on the Mount, who records Jesus's words with such care and clarity. Perhaps because he knew, in the marrow of his soul, what Jesus was describing. The Beatitudes weren't theory to him.

He knows what it means to be spiritually bankrupt. Matthew (that is, Levi, the son of Alphaeus) spent years chasing gain, but it left him hollow. His soul was dry, weary, grasping for something he could not name. And then—standing in the company of Christ—he found himself among the poor in spirit, those who have nothing left to offer but the emptiness they carry. And it is here, in this poverty, that the kingdom of heaven begins to open to him.

He mourns—not just the life he's left behind but the person he once was. He grieves the years lost to self-interest, the relationships sacrificed at the altar of profit. But he does not mourn without hope. At the feet of Jesus, his sorrow is not dismissed—it is received. And in that receiving, he is comforted with a peace he never expected to find.

He hungers. Not for silver anymore, not for status or security, but for something lasting—something real. He hungers for righteousness, for wholeness, for grace. And in Christ, that hunger is satisfied. Not by what he earns, but by what he's given: the mercy of a Savior who looks at him with love and calls him friend.

As we walk these Lenten days, we stand where Matthew once stood—beneath the mountain, listening. And we are challenged to believe that these strange blessings are not backward—they are the very shape of Christ's own heart. They are the map to Golgotha. And they are the key to Easter joy.

REFLECT

1. As a tax collector, Matthew likely experienced both the comfort of wealth and the shame of social rejection. How do your own experiences of injustice shape the way you hear and live out the Beatitudes?
2. Matthew mourned the life he left behind, but his mourning became a doorway to comfort in Christ. What losses or regrets in your life do you still need to grieve honestly so that they can be transformed by the Lord's mercy?

PRAY

LORD JESUS, YOU CALLED MATTHEW FROM HIS TABLE OF COINS TO THE RICHES OF YOUR KINGDOM. CALL ME FROM MY FALSE SECURITIES, AND TEACH ME THE FREEDOM OF POVERTY OF SPIRIT. RECEIVE MY MOURNING, SATISFY MY HUNGER, AND MAKE MY LIFE A LIVING RECORD OF YOUR MERCY. LET MY EVERY CALCULATION BE MEASURED BY YOUR LOVE. AMEN.

FIFTH WEEK OF LENT

SATURDAY

HE THEN IS EATEN UP WITH ZEAL FOR GOD'S HOUSE WHO DESIRES TO CORRECT ALL THAT HE SEES WRONG THERE. AND IF HE CANNOT CORRECT IT, HE ENDURES AND MOURNS. . . . LET ZEAL FOR GOD'S HOUSE CONSUME EVERY CHRISTIAN.

ST. AUGUSTINE

SIMON THE ZEALOT

Simon the Zealot must have burned with fury.

He had seen his homeland trampled, his people shamed, his God mocked by foreign rulers. He had heard the groans of the poor under Roman taxes, the cries of mothers watching soldiers drag away their sons. And something in him had cried out, "Enough!" Like so many others, Simon joined the cause of the Zealots—a movement born of pain, pride, and the desperate hope that violence might restore what had been lost.

His fire was real. His anger, justified. His longing for justice, sincere.

But then came Jesus.

And Jesus was nothing like the revolution he had imagined. He spoke of mercy. He taught, "Blessed are the peacemakers" (Mt 5:9). He healed the servant of a Roman centurion. He told Peter to put away his sword. And instead of waging war, he walked toward a Cross.

How hard must it have been for Simon to stay? How many times did his fists clench, his chest tighten, his old instincts scream to fight, to take control, to try to fix the world by force? But something deeper was happening, something breaking his heart even as it was being made new. Slowly, painfully, the fire that once burned to destroy was purified. Transformed.

Simon learns that the deepest courage is not in shedding someone else's blood but in giving his own. Real revolution happens not with rebellion but with surrender. He lays down his old weapons—not because he's weak but because he's stronger than ever, strong enough to follow the King whose throne is the Cross.

Lent reaches for the same places in us. The old wounds, the righteous anger, the desire to fix, control, correct. The fear that if we let go, all will be lost. But Christ invites us to follow, to trust that the way of mercy is not weakness but power, not foolishness but wisdom, not defeat but glory.

REFLECT

1. Simon's political zeal was fueled by real injustice and suffering. How do you discern when your own righteous anger is leading you toward Christ's way of mercy and when it is pulling you toward destructive paths?
2. Following Jesus forced Simon to lay down not only weapons but also deeply held strategies for changing the world. What strategies or habits of control are you still clinging to that are incompatible with the Gospel?
3. Jesus did not extinguish Simon's zeal—he transformed it. Where might God be asking to purify your passion so that it builds his kingdom instead of your own?

PRAY

LORD JESUS, YOU FOUND SIMON WITH A HEART BURNING FOR JUSTICE, FIERCE IN HIS RESOLVE TO SET THINGS RIGHT. YOU DID NOT EXTINGUISH HIS FIRE—YOU PURIFIED IT. TAKE MY OWN ANGER AT THE WORLD'S WRONGS, AND CLEANSE IT OF PRIDE AND VENGEANCE. WHEN MY FISTS CLENCH AND MY VOICE RISES, OPEN MY HANDS TO SERVE AND MY MOUTH TO BLESS. MAKE ME BRAVE IN YOUR WAY—THE WAY OF THE CROSS. AMEN.

HOLY WEEK

The Risen Christ

HOLY WEEK

PALM SUNDAY

A CUTTING FROM THE VINE PLANTED IN THE GROUND BEARS FRUIT IN ITS SEASON, OR A KERNEL OF WHEAT FALLING INTO THE EARTH AND BECOMING DECOMPOSED RISES AND IS MULTIPLIED BY THE SPIRIT OF GOD, WHO CONTAINS ALL THINGS. AND THEN, THROUGH THE WISDOM OF GOD, IT SERVES FOR OUR USE WHEN, AFTER RECEIVING THE WORD OF GOD, IT BECOMES THE EUCHARIST, WHICH IS THE BODY AND BLOOD OF CHRIST.

ST. IRENAEUS

SACRIFICE

Dostoevsky chose a single verse from scripture as the epigraph for *The Brothers Karamazov*: "Unless a grain of wheat falls into the earth and dies, it remains just a single grain; but if it dies, it bears much fruit" (Jn 12:24). Dostoevsky's sprawling tale of faith and doubt, guilt and redemption, is filled with characters who must decide whether they will let themselves be "planted" in sacrificial love.

On Palm Sunday, Jesus enters Jerusalem to shouts of "Hosanna" and the waving of palms. Yet St. John tells us that amid the crowd, "some Greeks" approach Philip and say, "Sir, we wish to see Jesus" (Jn 12:20–21). These Gentiles have come to the Temple to worship, but now they seek Christ himself. St. Thomas Aquinas sees in this moment a foreshadowing of the conversion of the nations. Even before the Cross, Jesus is gathering all peoples to himself.

When told of their request, Jesus responds with a solemn declaration: "The hour has come for the Son of Man to be glorified" (Jn 12:23). Their arrival signals that his mission is reaching its turning point. The glory he speaks of is not the fleeting glory of public praise—it is the glory of the Cross.

Then he gives us the image that Dostoevsky chose to frame his novel: the grain of wheat. If Christ, the grain of wheat, were to preserve his life, he would remain alone. But by surrendering himself to death, he becomes the source of a great harvest—the remission of sins, the conversion of nations, and the glory of eternal life. The "death" of the seed is not a loss of its power but a transformation, breaking open so that its life may be shared.

What's more, Christ does not speak of his own dying without speaking of ours: "Those who love their life lose it, and those who hate their life in this world will keep it for eternal life" (Jn 12:25). The "grain" is not simply Christ; it is every human heart.

If a person refuses to let go of pride, self-justification, and the illusion of control, he remains "alone," shut in on himself. But if he accepts the dying of self—laying down his life in love for God and neighbor—then his life becomes fruitful, capable of giving life to others.

And lest we shrink back, Christ makes a promise: "Where I am, there will my servant be also. Whoever serves me, the Father will honor" (Jn 12:26). The Father who glorified the Son will glorify those who follow him—not only in sharing his sufferings but also in sharing his resurrection life.

On Palm Sunday, the cheering crowd sees only the surface of glory. Jesus sees the field ready for planting and the furrow of the Cross before him. The seed will fall. The earth will close over it. And from that dark soil will spring a harvest beyond imagining.

REFLECT

1. In *The Brothers Karamazov*, the grain of wheat image becomes a lens for the characters' decisions—whether to cling to themselves or surrender in love. Where in your own life are you tempted to "remain alone" rather than be "planted" through humility, forgiveness, or service?
2. St. Irenaeus links the falling grain to the Eucharist—Christ's Body and Blood given for our nourishment. How does receiving the Eucharist invite you into the same pattern of self-giving love? What would it look like for you to live Eucharistically this Holy Week?

PRAY

LORD JESUS, YOU ARE THE GRAIN OF WHEAT BROKEN OPEN SO THAT THE WORLD MIGHT LIVE. PLANT MY LIFE DEEP IN THE SOIL OF YOUR WILL. BREAK OPEN MY PRIDE, MY SELF-RELIANCE, MY FEAR OF LOSS. TEACH ME TO LOVE WITH THE VULNERABILITY YOU EMBRACED ON THE CROSS, TRUSTING THAT IN EVERY SURRENDER, YOUR FATHER BRINGS FORTH LIFE. AMEN.

HOLY WEEK

MONDAY

WE WHO WISH TO BELONG TO THE CHURCH AND TO CELEBRATE THE PASSOVER WITH JESUS FOLLOW THAT MAN, WHOM I BELIEVE TO BE MOSES, GIVER OF THE LAW, WHO BEARS THIS KIND OF WATER, CARRYING SPIRITUAL DOCTRINE ABOUT IN HISTORICAL VESSELS.

ORIGEN

THE MAN WITH THE WATER JAR

"So he sent two of his disciples, saying to them, 'Go into the city, and a man carrying a jar of water will meet you; follow him'" (Mk 14:13). There's a strange detail here that we're likely to overlook. In first-century Jerusalem, carrying water was work typically done by women. Men didn't fetch water from the public well—certainly not in the middle of the day, and certainly not in plain view. It would have stood out to the disciples like a man in a pink raincoat on a sunny day.

So why was he there? Why was he carrying the jar? Was it a simple act of necessity—had he no wife or daughter to help him? Was he performing a servant's task out of duty? Out of kindness? Had he been asked? Had he been told?

We don't know. But we do know this: His task, his silent walk through the city streets, became part of the road to the Upper Room. And what's more, we should see in the water a powerful sign. Water is the beginning of the Christian life. Water is the sign of Baptism. Before Our Lord faced Gethsemane, before he offered his Body and Blood, water led the way.

Even if it wasn't typically a man's chore, it's a pedestrian and commonplace one. This man just carried a jar of water.

But what a weight it would have felt like, if he had known. What a holy burden—to carry something so ordinary, not knowing it was making way for the extraordinary. Not knowing that behind him would follow the footsteps of the apostles. That in the room he revealed, the Savior would kneel, would wash, would weep, would hand on love that endures to the very end.

Lent can feel like a season of silence. Of small things. Of prayers that no one sees. But the man with the water jar reminds us, as we begin Holy Week, that God works in the hidden things. Grace flows through the unnoticed. And sometimes the most sanctifying thing we can do is keep walking, keep carrying, even when we do not see the full picture.

REFLECT

1. The man's errand was ordinary—just carrying water—but it became a key link in the chain leading to the Last Supper. What daily routines, small acts of faithfulness, or unseen labors in your own life might be part of God's greater plan, even if you will never see the full fruit this side of heaven?
2. Water is the sign of Baptism, the beginning of the Christian life. Before Jesus could offer his Body and Blood, this water prepared the way. How does your baptism continue to shape your relationship with the Eucharist, and in what ways does the Lord still "lead you by water" into deeper communion with him?

PRAY

LORD JESUS, YOU CHOSE AN ORDINARY MAN WITH AN ORDINARY TASK TO LEAD THE WAY TO THE PLACE OF YOUR GREATEST GIFT. HELP ME TO SEE THAT NO ACT OF SERVICE IS TOO SMALL FOR YOUR PURPOSES. TEACH ME TO WALK FAITHFULLY EVEN WHEN I DO NOT SEE THE END OF THE ROAD, TO CARRY THE DAILY BURDENS YOU GIVE ME WITH PATIENCE AND LOVE, AND TO TRUST THAT YOU CAN MAKE EVEN THE SMALLEST OFFERING A STEP TOWARD THE EXTRAORDINARY WORK OF YOUR SALVATION. AMEN.

HOLY WEEK

TUESDAY

HE LOVED THEM SO MUCH THAT BY THAT VERY LOVE HE WOULD END HIS BODILY LIFE FOR A TIME AND SOON PASS FROM DEATH TO LIFE, FROM THIS WORLD TO THE FATHER. "GREATER LOVE HAS NO ONE THAN THIS, THAT HE SHOULD LAY DOWN HIS LIFE FOR HIS FRIENDS." AND SO, EACH PASSING OVER—THE ONE UNDER THE LAW AND THE OTHER UNDER THE GOSPEL—WAS CONSECRATED WITH BLOOD, THE FORMER WITH THE PASCHAL LAMB, THE LATTER WITH "CHRIST, OUR PASSOVER, WHO WAS SACRIFICED FOR US."

ST. BEDE

THE OWNER OF THE UPPER ROOM

A man had a guest room. A storeroom, perhaps—set apart, tucked above the noise of the street. And on the night of the Last Supper, it became the holiest room in the world.

One early tradition holds that the Upper Room belonged to the family of John Mark—the same Mark, the evangelist, who would later record the words "This is my body. . . . This is my blood." (Mk 14:22–24). Perhaps it was his mother's house. Perhaps he was there, watching from the stairs. We can only speculate. But what we do know is this: Someone in that household opened the door. Someone gave Jesus a place to stay.

What a contrast to Bethlehem, where Mary and Joseph were turned away. There was no room in the inn. The Word-made-flesh was born among animals and laid in a feeding trough. But now, as he prepares to offer his Body as the true Bread from heaven, Jesus is welcomed. The table is set. The guest room is open. Love finds shelter at last.

This Upper Room becomes more than a space for a meal. Here, the Eucharist is offered for the first time. Here, the basin and the towel are taken up, and the Teacher kneels to wash the feet of his friends. Here, the Great Commandment is spoken aloud: "Love one another . . . as I have loved you" (Jn 13:34). And after the Resurrection, it is here that the risen Lord returns. Here, behind locked doors, he offers his peace. And this same room trembles with wind and fire when the Holy Spirit descends at Pentecost.

Christ seeks a place—not in a room above the city but in our hearts. Too often, we echo Bethlehem: no room. We let the noise crowd him out, the distractions of work, fear, and hurry. But the one who was turned away at his birth now, in these final days of Lent, again asks, *Will you make a place for me?*

REFLECT

1. Bethlehem turned the Holy Family away; Jerusalem welcomed the Lord into an upper room. How does this contrast challenge you to examine the "availability" of your heart? Where have you let busyness, fear, or distraction crowd out your readiness to receive Jesus?
2. In that room, Jesus washed his disciples' feet, instituted the Eucharist, and spoke his Great Commandment of love. Which of these moments in the Upper Room do you most long to experience personally with the Lord, and why? How could you make more space in your daily life to live from that moment?
3. Tradition holds that the Upper Room later became the place of Jesus's post-Resurrection appearances and the descent of the Holy Spirit at Pentecost. Consider the spaces in your own life—both physical and spiritual—that the Lord might want to use again and again for his work. How can you keep them open to him?

PRAY

LORD JESUS, YOU FOUND A PLACE TO SHARE YOUR LAST MEAL, TO WASH THE FEET OF YOUR FRIENDS, TO POUR OUT YOUR LOVE IN THE EUCHARIST. I OPEN TO YOU THE ROOMS OF MY HEART. CLEAR AWAY WHAT KEEPS YOU OUT— MY SELFISHNESS, MY FEAR, MY DISTRACTIONS—AND DWELL IN ME AS YOU DID IN THAT UPPER ROOM. LET MY LIFE BE A PLACE WHERE YOUR LOVE IS WELCOMED, HONORED, AND SHARED. AMEN.

HOLY WEEK

WEDNESDAY (SPY WEDNESDAY)

O MADNESS! THE COVETOUSNESS OF JUDAS ALTOGETHER BLINDS HIM! HE HAD OFTEN SEEN JESUS WHEN HE WENT THROUGH THE MIDST AND DID NOT BETRAY HIM. JESUS HAD AFFORDED MANY DEMONSTRATIONS OF HIS GODHEAD AND POWER, AND NO ONE HAD LAID HOLD ON HIM. EVEN AT THE SUPPER JUDAS DID NOT CEASE TO TALK WITH HIM AND RECEIVE HIS CARE. THIS COULD HAVE PUT AN END TO HIS EVIL THOUGHT. BUT ALL THIS PROFITED NOTHING.

ST. JOHN CHRYSOSTOM

JUDAS ISCARIOT

Judas Iscariot was not an outsider or a stranger. He was chosen by Christ, named an apostle, sent out to preach, to cast out demons, to heal. The gospels never question his place among the disciples—he is always counted "one of the Twelve." He held the purse, administering the group's finances and needs. And it is precisely this closeness that makes his fall so painful. His betrayal is not the act of an enemy—it's the act of a friend.

At the Last Supper, Jesus shares bread with him. In the garden, he calls Judas "friend" (Mt 26:50). Even at the moment of the kiss that would hand Jesus over to death, the Lord does not curse him. He lets Judas come close. He receives the betrayal with a wounded, merciful heart.

Why did Judas fall?

The gospels suggest different layers of meaning: greed, disappointment, Satan's influence. Perhaps he hoped to force Jesus into a political revolution and grew disillusioned when the Messiah chose peace instead of power. Perhaps he never fully trusted Jesus's way of suffering love. Perhaps his vision of salvation was too small. Whatever the reason, he gave in to despair. When the silver coins no longer satisfied, and the weight of what he had done came crashing down, Judas tried to return the money. "I have sinned by betraying innocent blood," he said (Mt 27:3–4). But then, tragically, he believed the lie that his sin was beyond forgiveness.

He repented—but without saving hope.

How different from Peter, who also betrayed the Lord. Peter wept bitterly. But his sorrow led him back to Christ, and to mercy. Judas's sorrow turned him inward, and he saw only darkness.

This contrast is a warning for all of us. Even in our deepest falls, God's mercy is greater than our sin. No one is beyond redemption—unless we refuse to believe it.

REFLECT

1. Judas was not an outsider but one of the Twelve, entrusted with the group's finances and sent out to preach and heal. How does his closeness to Jesus challenge your assumptions about who can fall into sin? How does it invite you to watch over your own heart, even in seasons of apparent spiritual closeness?
2. Judas's betrayal was met not with curses but with the Lord's address of "friend," even in the act of betrayal. How might this reveal the depths of Jesus's mercy, and how does that mercy confront your own readiness (or reluctance) to forgive those who have wounded you?
3. Despair told Judas that his sin was beyond God's mercy. In what situations of your life, past or present, are you tempted to believe that lie? How can you root yourself more deeply in the truth that no sin is greater than God's willingness to forgive?

PRAY

LORD JESUS, YOU LOOKED ON JUDAS AS A FRIEND, EVEN IN THE MOMENT OF HIS BETRAYAL. GUARD ME FROM THE PRIDE THAT SAYS, "I COULD NEVER FALL." WHEN I DO SIN, DRAW ME QUICKLY BACK TO YOU, AND DO NOT LET DESPAIR CLOSE MY HEART TO YOUR MERCY. TEACH ME TO TRUST IN THE HOPE THAT NEVER DISAPPOINTS AND TO PROCLAIM WITH MY LIFE THAT YOUR LOVE IS GREATER THAN MY SIN. AMEN.

HOLY WEEK

HOLY THURSDAY

A TOO CAREFUL MANAGEMENT OF ONE'S INCOME, A TOO NEAR CALCULATION OF ONE'S EXPENSES—THESE ARE HABITS NOT EASILY LAID ASIDE. YET TO ESCAPE THE EGYPTIAN WOMAN JOSEPH HAD TO LEAVE HIS GARMENT WITH HER. AND THE YOUNG MAN WHO FOLLOWED JESUS HAVING A LINEN CLOTH CAST ABOUT HIM, WHEN HE WAS ASSAILED BY THE SERVANTS HAD TO THROW AWAY HIS EARTHLY COVERING AND TO FLEE NAKED. . . . AS LONG AS WE ARE CAUGHT UP IN THE THINGS OF THIS WORLD—WHILE OUR HEARTS ARE TIED DOWN BY POSSESSIONS AND INCOME—WE CAN'T THINK FREELY ABOUT GOD.

ST. JEROME

THE YOUNG MAN WHO FLED

"A certain young man was following him, wearing nothing but a linen cloth. They caught hold of him, but he left the linen cloth and ran off naked" (Mk 14:51–52). Some say he is Mark the Evangelist—young at the time of Jesus's Passion, perhaps too young to be counted among the Twelve, but close enough to have followed the events of that terrible night. If this is true, then the fleeing figure becomes a signature of humility: Mark inserts his own failure into the Gospel record, not to shame himself, but to point to the mercy of the one who restores us all.

Others suggest he is the rich young man from an earlier scene in the gospels—the one who ran up to Jesus, asking what he must do to inherit eternal life. Jesus, looking on him with love, told him to sell what he had, give to the poor, and follow. But the young man went away sorrowful, unwilling to let go. Could this linen cloth be all he had left?

Still others propose Lazarus, whom Jesus had raised from the dead. The linen garment, they say, might be the burial cloths still clinging to him. His presence in the garden, then, would speak of gratitude and loyalty, even if not yet courage.

And then there are those who wonder if it is John the Beloved, the youngest of the apostles, who reclined on Jesus's breast at the Last Supper. Full of love but not yet of age, quick to follow but not yet ready to stand firm.

Whoever the young man was, he represents something raw and real in us all. But his story doesn't end there.

Mark's gospel closes with another young man. This time, he is not running—he is sitting in the empty tomb. Clothed in a white robe, he says to the women, "Do not be afraid. He is risen." The two young men are echoes of one another—failure transformed by grace. The one who once ran now proclaims resurrection. The linen of shame becomes the robe of glory.

That is the promise of Lent. Wherever we've run, whatever we've left behind—Christ still calls us back. He takes our nakedness, our shame, our weakness, and clothes us in his mercy.

REFLECT

1. Whoever this young man was—Mark, Lazarus, John, or another—he followed Jesus into danger but fled when the cost became too high. When have you begun to follow Christ with zeal, only to retreat when obedience demanded more than you expected?
2. The Gospel of Mark begins with this young man fleeing naked and ends with another young man in a white robe announcing the Resurrection. How has God transformed your own failures into testimonies of his grace?

PRAY

LORD JESUS, I SEE MYSELF IN THE YOUNG MAN WHO RAN AWAY, CLINGING TO WHAT HE THOUGHT HE NEEDED. STRIP FROM ME THE FEARS, ATTACHMENTS, AND SELF-PROTECTIONS THAT KEEP ME FROM FOLLOWING YOU. CLOTHE ME INSTEAD WITH THE WHITE ROBE OF YOUR MERCY, SO THAT MY FAILURES MAY BECOME SIGNS OF YOUR VICTORY. AMEN.

HOLY WEEK

GOOD FRIDAY

WHEN THE CENTURION SAW WHAT HAPPENED, HE GLORIFIED GOD. HE SAID, "TRULY THIS MAN WAS RIGHTEOUS." PLEASE OBSERVE THAT IMMEDIATELY AFTER CHRIST ENDURED THE PASSION ON THE CROSS FOR US, HE BEGAN TO WIN MANY TO THE KNOWLEDGE OF THE TRUTH. IT SAYS, "WHEN HE SAW WHAT HAPPENED, THE CENTURION GLORIFIED GOD SAYING, 'TRULY THIS MAN WAS RIGHTEOUS.'"

ST. CYRIL OF ALEXANDRIA

LONGINUS, THE ROMAN CENTURION

The Roman centurion was no stranger to crucifixion. He had likely overseen countless executions, watching condemned men writhe in agony, curse their fate, and eventually fall silent under the weight of death. But something was different this time. This one didn't resist. This one forgave.

The centurion stood watch beneath the Cross. Duty kept him there—but something deeper began to stir. And as the sky went dark and the earth shook beneath Golgotha, the centurion stood still, shaken by what he had seen.

One of the soldiers took his spear and pierced the side of the crucified Christ. From that wound, blood and water flowed—life spilling out even in death. And in that moment, something happened in the heart of the centurion. A man trained to kill saw the truth of a love stronger than death: "Truly this man was God's Son" (Mk 15:39).

On this most solemn of days, when the Church stands still before the Cross, we join him—this soldier who saw what so many others missed. He had not followed Jesus. He had not heard the sermons or seen the signs. But he stood beneath the Cross, and he believed.

Good Friday is not a day of explanation. It is a day of silence, of awe, of confession. There is only Christ, crucified. Only the Lamb who takes away the sins of the world. Only his pierced side, still pouring out mercy.

The Church has long seen in the blood and water from Christ's side a sign of the sacraments—Baptism and the Eucharist, the very life of the Church. In the centurion, we glimpse the first soul drawn to that fountain of mercy. And we, like that centurion, are left to look up in wonder, to say, "Truly this man was God's Son!"

REFLECT

1. The blood and water from Christ's side symbolize Baptism and the Eucharist—the life of the Church. How do these sacraments continue to shape you, and how do you prepare your heart to receive them with awe rather than routine?
2. Standing at the foot of the Cross, the centurion saw what others missed. What in your life keeps you from standing still before Christ's sacrifice, allowing yourself to be moved by the truth of his love?

PRAY

LORD JESUS, ON THE CROSS YOU REVEALED A LOVE STRONGER THAN DEATH. LET ME STAND WITH THE CENTURION BENEATH YOUR PIERCED SIDE, RECEIVING THE MERCY THAT FLOWS FROM YOUR HEART. GIVE ME THE GRACE TO SEE YOU CLEARLY, TO CONFESS YOU BOLDLY, AND TO LIVE EACH DAY IN THE LIGHT OF YOUR SAVING LOVE. AMEN.

HOLY WEEK

HOLY SATURDAY

IT WOULD NOT HAVE SUFFICED FOR THE CHIEF PRIESTS, SCRIBES AND PHARISEES TO HAVE CRUCIFIED THE LORD OUR SAVIOR IF THEY HAD NOT ALSO GUARDED THE TOMB, CALLED IN THE MILITARY, SEALED THE ENTRANCE AND, AS FAR AS THEY WERE ABLE, RESISTED THE RESURRECTION. THEIR CONCERN FOR THESE DETAILS SERVES ONLY TO ADVANCE OUR FAITH; THE GREATER THEIR PRECAUTIONARY CARE, THE MORE FULLY IS REVEALED THE POWER OF THE RESURRECTION.

ST. JEROME

THE GUARDS AT THE TOMB

Roman soldiers—trained, hardened, unshaken—were assigned to watch a sealed tomb. A stone, a wax seal, a posted guard: the best security the world could offer.

They kept their watch in silence, unaware that beneath their feet, the earth was stirring. Unaware that the Crucified One—the one they had seen mocked, scourged, pierced—had descended into the place of the dead, not as a victim but as a conqueror.

They stood guard over a tomb while the King of Glory emptied the underworld.

They did not know that at that very hour, the Son of God was grasping the hand of Adam, lifting him from the dust. They could not see him speak light into the darkness, or witness his cross raised high like a banner in hell. They were blind to the splendor breaking into Sheol, deaf to the cry: "Sleeper, awake! Rise from the dead, and Christ will shine on you" (Eph 5:14).

These soldiers saw only stone.

But when the appointed time came—when the earth trembled and the angel rolled back the stone—these mighty men fell like the dead. Because the dead were waking. Because Christ, who had gone down into the grave, was rising from it.

They thought they were guarding a body. But they were keeping watch at the edge of a new creation.

They were witnesses—terrified, unknowing—of a love stronger than death. And though they fled in fear, though they did not understand, their watch became part of the greatest story ever told.

REFLECT

1. The guards at the tomb thought they were keeping watch over a dead body, unaware Christ was harrowing hell—setting captives free. How might this mystery change the way you view Holy Saturday moments in your own life, when all seems silent but God is still moving?
2. The soldiers fled in fear, missing the joy of the Resurrection. What fears might cause you to turn away from the new life Christ is offering, and how can you ask him for the courage to remain and see his glory?

PRAY

LORD JESUS, YOU SHATTERED THE SILENCE OF THE GRAVE AND BROUGHT LIGHT TO THOSE WHO DWELT IN DARKNESS. IN THE QUIET OF MY OWN WAITING, HELP ME TO TRUST THAT YOU ARE AT WORK. ROLL AWAY THE STONES IN MY HEART, AND LET ME STAND FIRM IN HOPE UNTIL THE DAWN OF YOUR RESURRECTION BREAKS UPON ME. AMEN.

HOLY WEEK

EASTER SUNDAY

BE THE FIRST TO SEE THE STONE TAKEN AWAY, AND PERHAPS YOU WILL SEE THE ANGELS AND JESUS HIMSELF. SAY SOMETHING. HEAR HIS VOICE. IF HE SAYS TO YOU, "DO NOT TOUCH ME," STAND FAR AWAY. REVERENCE THE WORD, BUT DO NOT GRIEVE BECAUSE HE KNOWS THOSE TO WHOM HE APPEARS FIRST.

ST. GREGORY OF NAZIANZUS

THE RISEN CHRIST

Peter and John have just run to the tomb. They've seen the linen wrappings, the stone rolled away. St. John tells us they believe—but then they simply go home.

Mary Magdalene doesn't. She lingers.

She remained at the foot of the Cross, and she remains at the tomb still.

It's not hard to picture her—shoulders shaking, eyes red, trying to peer through tears into the darkness. And then, something unexpected: Two angels are sitting where Jesus's body had been—one at the head, one at the foot. The angels ask, "Woman, why are you weeping?" (Jn 20:13). It's a gentle question. They know her sorrow is misplaced. But Mary is still too deep in grief to understand. She turns—and there he is. Jesus himself. Only, she doesn't recognize him.

St. John Chrysostom thinks Jesus hid his glory so as not to overwhelm her. Mary assumes he's the gardener—which, as St. Gregory points out, is truer than she realizes. Jesus is indeed the Gardener of her soul, tending the seeds he's planted in her heart.

And then, everything changes.

He says her name: "Mary." That's it. Just her name.

She knows instantly—this is the Lord she's been looking for. In that one moment, grief turns to joy, despair to hope. She wants to hold on to him, but Jesus tells her not to cling just yet—he has not yet ascended to the Father. The Resurrection changes everything. From now on, her relationship with him will be through faith, in the Spirit.

The church fathers see Mary as a model for every Christian who longs for Christ. In fact, our holy desires grow stronger when delayed. If our longing fades when God seems slow to answer, it isn't love at all. Mary teaches us to keep looking, to stay when others go home, to believe there's more to see.

And isn't that Easter in a nutshell?

The Resurrection isn't just a fact—it's an encounter. It's hearing your name spoken by the risen Lord. It's the moment when the Gardener turns to you and reveals the promise of transformation and life in its full, stupendous, mind-blowing glory.

There are seasons when Christ feels absent, when prayers seem to bounce back unanswered. But Easter says: Stay. Look again. Wait for him.

Because he's closer than you think.

REFLECT

1. The angels' question—"Why are you weeping?"—gently exposed Mary's misplaced sorrow. What griefs, fears, or disappointments might you be holding on to that the risen Lord wants to transform into joy?
2. Mary did not recognize Jesus at first. Are there ways you might be missing his presence in the ordinary "gardeners" and daily circumstances of your life?
3. Jesus calls Mary by name, and that changes everything. How have you experienced God speaking personally to you? Where do you need to hear him call your name again?

PRAY

RISEN LORD, YOU CALLED MARY BY NAME AND REVEALED THE TRIUMPH OF YOUR RESURRECTION. CALL EACH OF US BY NAME SO THAT WE MAY RECOGNIZE YOUR PRESENCE EVEN WHEN WE DO NOT SEE YOU CLEARLY. WHEN FAITH GROWS WEARY OR YOU SEEM DISTANT, GIVE US THE COURAGE TO REMAIN, TO WAIT, TO LOOK AGAIN, TO FIND THAT YOU ARE NEAR. AMEN.

NOTES

NOTES

NOTES

NOTES

FR. PATRICK MARY BRISCOE, OP, is a Dominican friar and author. He is promoter general for social communication for the Order of Preachers and a host of the *Godsplaining* podcast. A sought-after preacher and speaker, he has written widely on faith, culture, and the spiritual life, sharing the beauty of the Gospel with clarity and joy.

Briscoe earned a licentiate in moral theology degree from the Pontifical Faculty of the Immaculate Conception at the Dominican House of Studies in Washington, DC. Following his ordination, he served as a chaplain and theology instructor at Providence College and as a parish priest at St. Pius V Catholic Church in Providence, Rhode Island.

He currently resides in Rome, Italy.

godsplaining.org
Facebook: @patrickmaryop
X: @PatrickMaryOP
Instagram: @PatrickMaryOP

JONATHAN ROUMIE is a Catholic actor known for his role as Jesus in *The Chosen* series.